The Art of Creative Thinking™

By Gerard I. Nierenberg

BARNES
& NOBLE
BOOKS
NEW YORK

Foreword to the 1996 Edition

Having a good idea gives you a wonderful feeling. Trying to get a good idea can be grueling, frustrating labor.

Think back to the last time you came up with a good idea. Was it a stroke of genius? Was it a happy accident?

Unfortunately, that's not good enough. Your job and life requires you to solve problems and come up with new ideas. You cannot afford to wait passively for "something" to happen. You must make things happen.

Here is a system which makes sure that your creativity is placed under your conscious control. *The Art of Creative Thinking* shows you a structured, organized approach to being an "idea person." You'll gain specific, practical skills for getting the idea you need, when you need it. Once learned, every one of your problems becomes an opportunity to a degree that will delight you.

Creativity is commonly considered to be a mysterious element possessed by a select, "gifted" few. The fact is everyone is gifted with creative power, but for some the gifts have become dormant.

Learn how to preserve your child-like thinking skills. To a child every problem demands a new solution. But as we grow older, we develop thinking patterns and habits. We attempt to use previously successful solutions for every problem—whether they work or not.

This book will help you reverse that process. In learning these techniques, you will realize that creative thinking is not tedious or complex. It is not a burden, or something to sweat over. In fact it is disarmingly simple—almost second nature—if you allow it to be.

The Art of Creative Thinking will help you be a better creative person in every way. It is your competitive edge. You will learn to:

- Overcome creative blocks with forced flashes of insight (... how often have you missed deadlines or settled for second-best ideas just because your creativity wasn't "flowing" at the time?)
- Organize your creative impulses into a systematic approach (... do you haphazardly search for creative solutions? ... become frustrated when your random methods don't yield results?)
- Expand and refine your creative ideas (... how many of your potentially "hot" ideas have gone stale because you lost enthusiasm or failed to "work out the kinks?")
- Sell your ideas confidently and convincingly (... you know your idea is good, but no one will buy it. What's wrong?)
- See your ideas through to fruition (... how many of your ideas never got off the drawing board? ... or lost their power in the translation?")

A failure to summon your creativity comes in many guises. Executives call it "stagnation." Authors call it "writer's block." Artists call it "a blank."

I call it "Creative Shock"—when people's minds get stuck in a rut. When the well runs dry, most people become helpless or retreat to familiar approaches (which are usually no longer effective).

Creative blocks can be overcome! With the approaches presented in this book, you will be able to systematically work your way through your "think-maze" and force intuitive flashes that produce results.

This book is filled with stories, examples, exercises, experiments, and problems that will keep your creative skills going. It will help you tap your unlimited creative potential on an ongoing basis. You will refer to it over and over to get your creative energy going.

—*Gerard I. Nierenberg*

Contents

6 THE ART OF CREATIVE THINKING

Your Tools for Creative Thinking

Many remain unskilled by
finding fault with their tools.

Gerard Nierenberg

Author's Comment

This book will help you understand how, by changing the position of the light, you can "see" an object differently (as a square, a circle, and a triangle). It demonstrates our potential to creatively see the world anew.

Would you have difficulty imagining a square peg that fits into round and triangular holes? (See diagram at end of Introduction.)

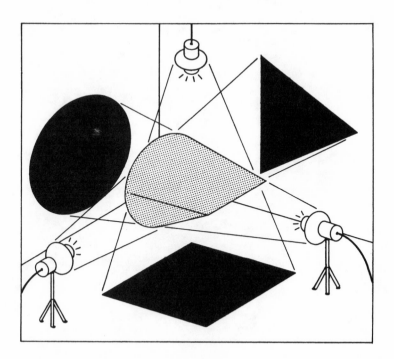

Figure 1

Introduction: Purpose of This Book, Definition of Creativity

Heaven and earth, center and circumference were made in the same instant of time, and clouds full of water, and man was created by the Trinity on the 26th of October, 4004 B.C., at 9 o'clock in the morning.
—John Lightfoot, 1654

Some people have tried to tell us with misplaced precision exactly where and when a creative act took place. Even more presumptuous, others have been second-guessers—they could have done it better.

Had I been present at the Creation, I would have given some useful hints for the better ordering of the universe.
Alfonso X (called the Wise), king of León and Castile (1221-1284)

There have always been attempts to gain insight into a creative act, but rarely has anyone ever tried to delve into the *how* of creative thinking.

The purpose of this book is to show you *how*, by thinking in certain ways, you can solve your problems creatively. Problems exist in all shapes and sizes—and in every aspect of life. Creative thinking is what is needed to provide alternative solutions to every problem you have—from the smallest to the largest. Once you have read and studied this book, few if any difficulties will resist your creative solutions. Instead of obstacles, problems will present opportunities to exercise your creative thinking to a degree that will delight you.

Consider how you have related to creativity in the past. Can you recall when you were last creative? Can you recognize creativity in yourself and others, or is it a mysterious element possessed only by geniuses? If you have difficulty answering these questions, it may be that you fail even to recognize a creative experience. Can you think creatively whenever you want to? Or do you have to wait for a happy accident to line things up just the way you need them? If you must, then you are not realizing your full creative potential.

Creative thinking, broadly defined, means coming up with something new. It is part of human thinking skills. These are the skills that have insured human survival, therefore cultural continuum (civilization) and growth. This working definition of creativity includes the masterworks of art and science as well as a new recipe invented by a homemaker.

As infants we began to think creatively. Each situation was new and had to be handled in a new (creative) way. Whether we ascribe this talent, as the child observer Jean Piaget did, to the interaction of our inborn predispositions, or as Noam Chomsky, the observer of language did, to inborn properties of the mind, we survived, which proves our creativity. As our experience grew and we continued to deal with new things successfully, behavioral patterns developed. With maturity, as new situations occurred, we handled them with previously successful thinking patterns rather than by trying to find new solutions. In other words, we had become hidebound and had forgotten how to be creative. Most of us continue this behavioral pattern throughout our adult life.

Studies demonstrate that we utilize only about ten percent of our brain capabilities. These studies also indicate that we can develop mental talents almost without limit.

This book will offer you methods to develop your creative thinking and substantially increase your mental capacities. The methods employ the use of the creative thinking skills which are divided into five areas of use: (1) knowing differences (making structures), (2) knowing similarities (making relations), (3) knowing changes (making order), (4) knowing and changing levels and (5) knowing and changing points of view.

To help you gain new insights, this book will provide you with problems to solve, tests to take, and workshop exercises and applications.

Creative thinking skills can be used as search patterns of your past experiences. With these techniques you can review and revive all conscious and even subconscious memories that might have even a remote relevance and discover new solutions to present problems.

Although these mental skills are not difficult to master, the problem is first to be able to identify, separate and objectify the tools, and then to bring them under conscious use and control. This book shows you how to do that. Once the fallacies and mysteries are stripped away, you will see the creative process for what it is: the means of achieving new solutions to any problem that may confront you. You will be utilizing creativity for *results*—and not necessarily to understand the forces behind it. Lack of talent, inspiration, interest or even the distastefulness of a situation will no longer serve as an excuse to limit your choices. You may even find yourself with the happy-go-lucky attitude of King Taufaahau Topou IV of Tonga, who in 1977 had a double problem: in spite of the fact that one of his subjects' prized national foods was fruit bats, there were too many of them. Fruit bats were destroying their crops, and therefore, they were short of exports. Instead of admitting failure, the king paid an official visit to nearby Guam and set up a sales force to boost Guam's consumption of fruit bats. This would increase Tonga's total exports and eliminate a lot of bats. The king of Tonga had found a creative solution which for him had been a literally distasteful problem. He explained, "I don't go head over heels for fruit bats." Our rewards come not from having brains, but in using them.

CREATIVE THINKING
SKILLS PROBLEM WORKSHOP

This exercise is designed to help you assess your *present* creative thinking skills. It is anticipated that after you finish this book, you will discover that by applying your expanded creative skills, you will find many more new creative solutions to the problem in the following workshop exercise. However, to make it relevant and not bias the exercise, supply a real problem for which you are seeking a solution.

Before reading the balance of the book:

State a problem in several lines for which you would want some creative solutions. (Examples: How to perform your work more efficiently; how to improve your income; how to aid poor vision.)

Now list, in brief sentences, all creative solutions for the problem you can think of. (When finished, draw a line under the last solution.)

The Creative Thinking Skills Problem Workshop Conclusion at the end of the book will return to your problem and solutions. Do the conclusion only after you have finished reading the book.

You will find that after reading this book and mastering its methods, the conclusion of this workshop will show you that you are then capable of finding many more solutions of which you are not now aware. Your creative horizons will be expanded.

EXERCISE

How to Make as Well As See a Square Peg That Fits into Round and Triangular Holes

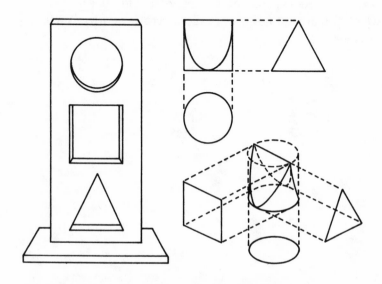

What mental changes do we make to accept changing structures (labels)? "It is square, round, triangular."

1

You Control Your Creative Thinking Skills

Failure to use such an abundant inherent treasure as creativity, whether it be because of unawareness that it exists, indifference, or deliberate stultification is more than a waste; it is self-betrayal.

—Masatoshi Yoshimura

Creativity has been defined in different ways. Dr. Edward Land, (the Polaroid camera inventor, described it as "the sudden cessation of stupidity," and Dr. Margaret Mead said, "To the extent that a person makes, invents or thinks something that is new to him, he may be said to have performed a creative act." For our purposes, this definition is useful: When a human being does something that is new for that person, he or she is being creative. Every individual has the potential for creating *new* ideas, relationships and objects among the many possibilities in life. For some, creativity is a conscious act, for others, an accident, and for still others it seems an impossibility.

The word "new" is explicit or implied in most definitions of creativity. To some, the unknown gives an element of mystery to the act. This is charmingly illustrated in an ancient parable of India: °

"A constant source of mystery for dragonfly nymphs in a pond is what happens to them when, on reaching the age of chrysalis, they pass through the surface of the pond never to

---

° Walter Sullivan, "Hole in the Sky," from *The New York Times Magazine*, July 14, 1974.

return. Each nymph, as it feels impelled to break through the pond's surface, promises to return and tell those who remain behind what really happens, and to confirm or deny a rumor attributed to a frog that when a larva emerges on the other side of the world, it becomes a marvelous creature with a long slender body and iridescent wings. But on emerging from the surface of the pond as a fully formed dragonfly, the transformed nymph is unable to penetrate the surface no matter how much it tries and how long it hovers. The nymphs left behind can only lament: 'Will none of you in pity to those you left behind disclose the secret?' "

Like the dragonfly nymphs, we tend to see any act that transforms something old into something new as a fait accompli—a finished product that appears as if by magic. We are delighted with the results but feel no obligation to duplicate or even understand them. After all, the whole thing has taken place outside our natural element. How could we be expected to understand? It is a surprise, an accident.

Suppose, instead of viewing creativity as an accident, we see it as a process—a logical progression of ideas and mental images that can transform the elements of reality into something new. We know we can do this in the physical world. We can combine two elements—hydrogen and oxygen, for example—and from two gases produce a liquid. Is it not possible to create new concepts from the vast mental lumberyard that each of us possesses? It's not only possible, it is constantly being done before our eyes.

Let us dismiss once and for all the myth that creative people are geniuses and that only geniuses are creative. We do expect geniuses to have talent, ability, intelligence, alertness and perseverance. We are also inclined to think that if we do not have these desirable qualities to a high degree we cannot be creative. In fact, however, none of them is essential to the creative thinking skills. If they were, the human race as we know it today would not have advanced to its present cultural state. Those desirable qualities of genius are not that abundant.

Geniuses do share two attributes with other creative individuals: flexibility and adaptability. However, who could be more flexible and adaptable than little children? They have to be. Literally, their survival depends upon it. They constantly must come up with new (to them) solutions to many problems every single day. They are, therefore, enormously creative.

With this in mind we can now consider a discussion of creativity as a process. E. W. Sinnott in "The Creativeness of Life °" places it in perspective: "Just as the organism pulls together, at random, formless stuff into a patterned system of structure and function of the body, so the conscious mind seems to select and arrange and correlate these ideas and images into a pattern. The resemblance between the two processes is close.The concept is worth considering that the organizing power of life, manifest in mind as in body—for the two are hardly separable—is the truly creative element. Creativity thus becomes an attribute of *life."*

Just as we can study the sequential development of the dragonfly from egg nymph to flying insect, we can trace the normal sequential development of a child's mental and motor abilities that continuously help the infant solve new problems (and be creative). The mystery of both processes can be eliminated by comparison and analysis. The wonder and joy of creativity, however, will be heightened, for you will be freed of a tremendous burden. Creativity will no longer be seen as an accident or act of genius, but your conscious understanding and deliberate exercise of familiar skills.

The famous writer James Joyce, concerned about the mental illness of his daughter who was schizophrenic, consulted psychoanalyst Carl Jung. Jung described the daughter's rambling as free access to her unconscious mind. Joyce was famous for his stream-of-consciousness technique in which he

---

° E. W. Sinnott, "The Creativeness of Life," *Creativity and Its Cultivation*, ed. H. H. Anderson (New York: Harper and Row, 1959).

tried to blend subjective and objective reality. Aware that many regarded his books as little more than the ranting of a madman, he wondered aloud what the difference was between his own and his daughter's use of words. Jung replied, "You mastered the intellectual dive, she falls."

Most of us, through lack of understanding and disuse, have permitted our creative thinking skills to fall. As with James Joyce, we can guide and control these skills to utilize the creative process fully.

2

Recreate Your Childhood Creative Thinking Skills

A childlike man is not a man whose development has been arrested; on the contrary, he is a man who has given himself a chance of continuing to develop long after most adults have muffled themselves in the cocoon of middle age habit and convention.
— Aldous Huxley, "Vulgarity in Literature"
Music at Night, 1931

"Spontaneous" creativity—which many people regard as the *only* kind—is child's play. Children must have an inexhaustible ability to think, do and say things that are new, fresh and even quite unexpected. For the average adult, much of the charm about childhood creativity lies in its seeming effortlessness and spontaneity. Similarly, many adults are inclined to regard a baby's lot as a very soft one—no work, no worries—"all he does is eat and sleep." One New York politician understood it was not that simple. Asked if he was worried about the tough election campaign he faced, he replied: "No. I sleep like a baby. I sleep for an hour and wake up crying."

Shakespeare's "All the World's a Stage" in *As You Like It* neatly summed up what we see around us: the *physical* development of mankind from infancy to old age. We all have a fairly clear idea of how a child changes physically and how his motor skills develop as he matures. It has been only in recent years, however, that we have begun to sense how a child's mind develops. This may be the reason why we have had such an unclear idea of how the creative thinking skills work.

The development of a child's mind is an enormously complex subject. To put it in perspective, consider the gold medal awarded Andrew H. Bobeck in 1977 by the Danish Academy of Technical Sciences. The award was in recognition of Bobeck's work of twenty years in developing what are called magnetic bubble memories. In their first practical test, four magnetic bubble memory chips, with a total capacity of 272,-000 binary digits of information (either zero or one), were coded to produce twelve seconds of speech. One message (produced for a Detroit telephone exchange) was "We're sorry. You have reached a nonworking number." How much more memory is needed by a child's working mind!

You can further understand what an infant must achieve if you imagine that you have lived in isolation for the past nine months. Then suddenly you are transported to Times Square during the evening rush hour. How well would you cope with the sudden rush of sensory details? Could you bring order to the chaos of sights, sounds, smells, tastes? Would you panic when the jostling crowd surrounded you?

No matter how badly you might react, you still have an advantage over a newborn baby. Why? Because over the years you have established certain thought patterns that permit you to deal with (to structure, relate and order) the confusing mass of objects around you. Looking at a sign above your head you can even assign the scene a label: Times Square.

A baby's mind cannot yet do that. It takes time—years, actually—for the baby to grasp the concepts that make mature creative thinking possible. Simplistically stated, prompted by its own desires and needs and by responding to the varied impulses of the surrounding environment, the baby develops ordered thoughts. This ordering process is far from simple. Guy Murchie puts it this way: "Should you glance for just one second upon an ordinary yellow dress, the electrons in the retinas of your eyes must vibrate about 500,000,000,000,000 times during that interval, registering more oscillation in that second than all the waves that have beat upon all the shores of all the earthly oceans in ten million years." This ordering of impulses is at the primary level of sensation. The infant also begins to structure a confusing mass of sensory impressions. It realizes a crib is not a mother. A breast is not a thumb. Further, it relates its mother's arms and a crib. Both offer comfortable places to sleep. And breasts and thumbs are related and structures that satisfy the desire to suck. William James wrote of this process that cognitive life begins when one is able to exclaim, "Hello! Thingumabob again."

Thus, even in very early life, a child is mentally far ahead of the binary computer. Instead of questions that can be answered by zero-one, there is understanding of more subtle questions: How can I structure it? How can I order it? What relationships exist? These questions must then be answered on a level that serves the infant. The result will not be a nine-second message, moreover, but a potentially infinite number of responses to new problems. The selection of responses makes up the child's current *point of view*. In short, in dealing with new situations, babies use their creative thinking skills.

As children grow, they discover language, an additional mental technique that can help them continue to handle the new. One of the first and most obvious uses of language is to provide labels. This increases our use and understanding of structure, order and relation. For example, a man handed a Philadelphia bank teller a note. The teller announced rather nastily that he couldn't read his writing. So the man said, "I'm a bank robber." The man behind him said, "I'm a policeman." The would-be robber gave up immediately and was arrested without a struggle.

The three labels in this story—teller, bank robber and policeman—could give a developing child an idea of the social level, structure, order and relation of a particular group in 'Philadelphia in the 1970's and might even lead to a creative idea: I'll join the police when I grow up, or I will learn to write more legibly. For most adults, however, labeling loses its rich creative ability. In this case the robber seems limited to a computer either/or solution—if the game's up, give up.

It would be misleading to imagine the use of creative thinking skills as springing full-blown from an infant's mind. But just as a computer can be programmed to perform an infinite variety of tasks by using only the zero-one options, so the human mind seems to perceive "reality" through point of view, a tripartite decision about how to structure, order and relate on many different levels. For example, we can grasp the idea of an atom (a point of view), a so-called building block of the physical universe (on a low level), by assigning a distinctive structure, order and relation to each of the various elements. Then we can go on mentally to a very high level to create an equally "logical" universe.

Even today you can find people taking opposite sides of this old question: Is a child born with its mind a clean slate? Some say yes; others, taking the view of Kant, feel that we bring into life with us certain concepts, such as time, space and causality. It is possible that as a result of the evolution of man's brain, people come into this world with certain abilities to think that are innately independent of their own experience (that is, they have a "slate," clean or not). This results from the structures and methods by which the sensory organs record sensations and the processes by which the brain utilizes them. Raw data is transformed into highly developed structures that are made in accord with the requirement and level of development of our brain. These are neurological transformations. The sensory information is changed into a system that can be used by the brain in accordance with its preexisting program. It is my contention that the system we are born with is our ability to think about the universe and recognize structure, order, relation, point of view and level—our creative thinking skills.

It might be said, therefore, that children are "predisposed" to use these five concepts in their analysis of the world around them. They do not use them efficiently at first, but well enough to come up with creative (new) solutions to their problems. As they grow, acquiring half their knowledge of the world before they are five, their perceptions of structure, order and relation and their use of skills at numerous levels are sharpened until, for most, a certain plateau of intellectual competence is reached. Except for the lucky few who continue to remain creative, the plateau may be the end of the line. For example, the mayor of a large city was asked to consider compulsory arbitration as a new solution. Reaching beyond his mental plateau for the familiar metaphor of a two-edged sword that can cut both ways, he stumbled and "created" a unique object, stating that arbitration was "a two-headed sword." Try to attack your problem by cutting both ways with *that* implement!

If you have reached a plateau where creativity no longer seems possible, it may be because you have unwittingly imposed limits on the skills that make up your point of view. It is time to consider this subsidiary thinking skill—point of view—in its most rudimentary form. Of course children have points of view: their own. They cannot see the world in any other way. However, they do not realize this. Even though the child sees structure, order and relation in ways that appear different from an adult looking at the same event, they do not yet feel that they have to make others agree. For example, young children four to six, according to Jean Piaget, believe that ten objects placed close together are less than ten more widely spaced apart. They also think that containers of a certain shape hold "more" than containers of the same volume but of another shape, even though they might empty one full container into the other and see that it, too, is filled exactly to the brim. They may suddenly realize that there are two kinds of children—boys and girls—only after they are two years old. The child's point of view is evolving toward mutual acceptance and is still open-ended.

Adults looking at children's art easily recognize the "primitive" developing elements in it. The child's point of view seems alien to adults. Yet adults should recognize that these are creative thinking accomplishments, not because of their strangeness but because the child has dealt with structure, order and relation from a point of view that is gradually developing and giving the child new insights. Your use of point of view can be a door to creativity which can be opened or closed.

A great paradox of creative thinking is that, when you have discovered a mental combination of structure, order and relation and have identified a pattern for the first time, thereafter each time you use an exact duplication of that pattern, you run the risk of its becoming less creative in coping with fresh experiences. As can be said, some things are clever only the first time. This happened to Henry Ford. He introduced the Model T in 1908 and stubbornly continued to turn out the same car until 1927. (He is supposed to have said the customer could have any color he wanted—so long as it was black.) The Ford Motor Company lost its preeminence because of this stubborn adherence to a once creative idea.

How can you avoid a similar fate? First, you must develop knowledge and understanding of your uses of the creative skills. Like most people, you probably base your understanding of these skills only on your initial childhood applications. This can be incapacitating. Second, you can understand and see how the skill of changing point of view can achieve great creative leverage. For example, in changing point of view you also change structure, order and relation. These are the first four mental tools at your disposal. You can reactivate your creative thinking skills by knowingly using them. Then you will not wait passively for "something" to happen. You will make things happen. You will preserve the "spirit" of a child and be creative.

EXERCISES

Children and Art

As an experiment, fold your hands and examine them. Note which thumb, the right or the left, is on top. It varies with different people. Whatever the cause, it is difficult to break out of the pattern. Now try placing your other thumb on top by changing the interlacing of *all* your fingers. If your hands feel uncomfortable, you are doing it correctly. This often happens when we change the habit pattern that has always worked in the past.

Drawing Exercise

The object of the following exercise is to move us first back to the age of six or seven when we made a transition in our creative thinking skills. Instead of drawing what we saw and felt, we started to draw our structures (symbols). Then when we could no longer make our symbols look like our conceptions of reality, we stopped drawing. This exercise will take you back and allow you to again continue to draw.

1. From memory, on the next page, draw a picture of the head of a person you know. Allow 15 minutes.

2. Note that this will show you the structures you have "on file" in your mind.

3. On page 30, now draw the drinking cup with the illusion of the same face on each of the stem sides, *using a face* from your own memory. If you are right-handed, draw the left profile first, then the other profile. If left-handed, vice versa. Look at the example below.

Note optical illusion of face silhouetted on each side of the stem.

When you have finished, read on:

4. The first face was easier; you produced it from your memory. The second face was more difficult to draw. The first face was drawn from the structures which you have on file in your memory. The second face was drawn by your ability to maintain relations. It was necessary to keep the relations of both sides the same.

5. You have now experienced how to break out of your structured mode and consider relations in your drawing.

6. We will now draw an upside-down picture, using one drawn by Pablo Picasso as our model to copy from.

   a. Allow 15 minutes for this drawing exercise.

   b. Do not look at the drawing you are copying with the right side up until you have finished.

   c. Cut out the page with the drawing and place it upside down, above the page you are to draw on. Look over the entire drawing. Notice the many relations of the lines. Observe both sides of the lines and the spaces between the lines.

   d. Start drawing from the top, allowing the lines to come together as the relations dictate.

   e. When completed turn your drawing right side up.

   f. Compare this drawing with the drawing you first made of the head. With instruction and practice, any adult can overcome the mental limits that we non-artists place on our drawing skill. The average adult has the skill of a twelve-year-old child.

For additional references see:
Nicolaïdes, Kimon, *The Natural Way to Draw.* Boston: Houghton Mifflin Co., 1969.
Edwards, Betty, *Drawing on the Right Side of the Brain.* Los Angeles: J.P. Tarcher, Inc., 1979.
Gardner, Martin, *The Ambidextrous Universe,* New York: Charles Scribner's Sons, 1979.

3

Using Your Creative Thinking Skills with Arts and Science

There are techniques of being intelligent. It is not easy to acquire the proper use of the mental tools which we have thoughtlessly inherited or which are implicit in the construction of our brains. Severe effort and long practice are required.   —Percy W. Bridgman

The Child is father of the Man.
—William Wordsworth

Gertrude Stein had a remarkable ability to make profound statements with deceptive simplicity. Her constant companion, Alice B. Toklas, recorded Stein's dying words: "What is the answer?" (Alice was silent.) "In that case, what is the question?"

If you are seeking a creative answer to your problem, you must first give sufficient attention to understanding what the problem is. As we have seen, the mind grasps the "reality" of an experience by structuring, ordering and relating it. Again, these terms are interdependent. We can no more "see" structure or order or relation separately than we can see only one of the three dimensions. However, without intellectually understanding each one, deeper perspective is lost. As students we accept that we are able to know the length of the equator without dealing with its thickness, the size of electrons depends on the condition of the experiment, or the size of a comet changes as it approaches the sun, even though its mass remains constant. Also just as defective vision can distort "reality," so the uninformed mind can give undue emphasis to structure, order or relation. This can impair your ability to understand what might occur and what the problem might be. Without full appreciation and understanding of the creative thinking process, you will find answers only by accident. So it is as important for the mind to have an integrated understanding of the terms structure, order and relation, and their uses, as it is for the eye to see length, breadth and depth for complete vision.

To state the problem of understanding reality another way, there are certain concepts in life that we accept as an integral whole. We know that they are made up of several interrelated factors that cannot be separated except mentally. If they are separated in the real world, they fail to exist. Knowledge, dimensions and color are a few such concepts. Through our concept of knowledge we know reality. We discover that knowledge consists of three basic elements: structure, order and relation. A comparison could be made between this discovery and our conceptualization of dimension: height, width and depth. We easily understand how difficult it is to see those elements completely separated. We do it by mentally separating the elements, for example, comparing only the height of human beings or mountains. We might want to know the precise height of Mt. Everest, but be content with "a lot of mountain" as an answer to its width and depth. We can have a concept of height alone, as we can of depth and width, but these concepts must in reality be supported by the other elements, even though they may not be relevant.

One way to show specifically the integration of the various elements of dimension is quite literally to do it with mirrors. When you stand in front of a mirror you will note that the left ear in the image is actually your right ear. You can confirm this by touching your ear with your right hand. That too is reversed in the mirror image. This incidentally is explained by a fundamental law of reflection: the angle of incidence is equal to the angle of reflection.

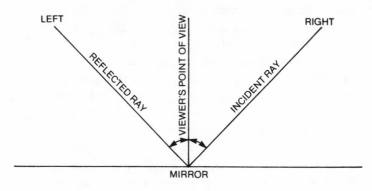

Figure 2

However, consider that, as shown in Figure 2, even though the mirror is flat or plane, we can see not only height and width, we seem to see depth. Actually, the image of the object appears to lie behind the mirror at a distance equal to the distance between the viewer and the mirror. Thus, we seem to see all three dimensions. An illusion in dimensions is necessary for the mirror to present a three-dimensional object on a two-dimensional surface. However, in achieving this illusion, reversals take place in other dimensions. If our ears are reversed, why, if you put your head on one shoulder isn't your chin where your forehead is and vice versa? The illusion if you reflect on it is more extensive than first appears. There are six different mirror images: two different mirror images for each of the three dimensions. Two image reversals take place in each of the three dimensions. In which one you look for reversal depends on your point of view. There are six different mirror images: all reverse left to right. Mirrors in front of and behind you will reverse depth (front to back). Mirrors overhead and underneath you will reverse in height. Mirrors along both sides of you will reverse in width. (Further illustrations are in Chapter 8 and Figures 8 and 9, pages 92 and 93.) The mirror's images overhead and underneath you reverse your chin and forehead.

The process of seeing colors is also conceptual. The eye is

synthetic—that is, incapable of seeing orange light as a combination of red and yellow lights. Once two or more colors are combined, a new color results. Again we can intellectually understand the process but cannot separate the parts perceptually.

To grasp the concept of knowing, basic to expanding our creative thinking, one should fully understand its components: structure, order and relation. These three terms make up our concept of knowledge—our reality. In order to expand our creativity, it is necessary to consider each of these terms individually and understand how in our own problem-solving we may habitually neglect one or more of them while we restrict ourselves to using the remaining factors over and over. The difficulties in understanding are the same as those involved in separating dimensions, mirror images and colors.

To understand these elements of knowledge and see their interrelations, we are forced to start on as basic a level of understanding as possible. At this lowest level the definitions are circular, or tautological: order is a structured relation, structure is a related order, relation is an ordered structure. Order deals with change, sequences in time and space. We can say a hand (structure) that differs from other structures is the arrangement (order) of the fingers, palm, etc. However, it has a similarity (relation with other hands). A piece of music (structure) is the sequence (order) of notes that are arranged in various ways such as by tonality or modality (relation). A grandfather (structure) and his grandson (structure) are related (the sequence of generations). They are structured on a still higher level to comprise the family.

The examples above are perhaps "true" but can offer only limited understanding. They fail to give sufficient insight because they are somewhat one-dimensional, like a one-legged stool. They lack the three-legged stability of the well-rounded skillful perceptions of mature, fully creative thinking. There are degrees of development of creative thinking. We see limited creativity without maturity in considering the first three types of children's painting. Elliot W. Eisner distinguishes *four* distinct types of creative children. The first he calls *boundary pushers* because "they always seem to want to push the limits of the ideas of objects." Their primary concern is in establishing *relations*. The second group he calls *aesthetic organizers* because their paintings show a "marked sense for aesthetic *order*." The third group are *inventors* who create "new objects *(structures)* by combining materials." Freud says: "Every child at play behaves like an imaginative writer in that he creates a world of his own, or more truly, he *rearranges* the things of his world and *orders* it in a new way that pleases him better." The first of Eisner's three groups discussed above are by Freud's definition creative children. They still differ from creative adults in that they only emphasize structure or order or relation at the expense of the other two (although their minds do not permit them to exclude them completely.)

Adults, on the other hand, who think creatively developed from and correspond to Eisner's fourth children's group: the *boundary breakers*. They reject "the assumptions that everyone else takes for granted and formulate new premises and proceed to develop a radically new system of thought." Here structure, order and relation are adequately considered and the result is not just a creative "child's painting" but a *mature* creative work.

Learning with maturity from children and going beyond to a thoroughly reasoned analysis of the structure, order and relation of any subject can provide deep insights into what "the question" is, and possibly give a creative answer. By the same technique, you can rearrange the mental building blocks to make a new (to you) structure, order and relation that will form a new answer. Both the question and the answer can serve as separate mental search fields and stimulate new solutions and actions.

Let us now consider two additional creative thinking skills: changing levels (for example, moving levels from macroscopic to the microscopic), and changing point of view (being able to see yourself and surroundings as others see them). Some of the infinite variety of perspectives (combined levels and point of view) that can be used include the ways painters create illusions of three-dimensional objects on flat surfaces. They change levels (they do not reverse dimensions as a mirror does). Worm's-eye perspective views the subject from below, frontal perspective views the object on the same level as the viewer, bird's-eye is of course from above. Aerial perspective takes advantage of the illusion that distant objects are less distinct in color and form than nearer ones. Time (which is order) can provide different points of view. Claude Monet painted fifteen different pictures of the same haystack at different times of day. The literal perspective of the haystack, in the formal sense of the word, is the same in all. By changing light (order), the fifteen pictures are radically different from each other.

You might ask: "Changing perspective might help in creating a painting, but what possible practical value does it have?" Or perhaps that can be rephrased: "I'm not a painter or a writer, what's in it for me to change perspective?" We have observed that children are *forced* to be creative. They must deal with events without the benefit of experience. In spite of everything, they grow up—physically, at least— and the changing life process has compelled them to be creative. Once the body, including the brain, has attained full growth, however, it is easy—even commonplace—for adults to declare a moratorium on creativity. They have not just "learned" from their experiences; they are frozen into them. However, the creative thinking skills used as search patterns will aid in the defrosting.

Can analyses of levels and points of view be of any practical use in enhancing creative thinking? Let's take a real-life situation. Eight major oil companies in the United States had quite understandably taken the position that vertical integration of their industry would maximize profits and minimize waste. Therefore, they created an industry that controlled pumping, transportation, refining and sale of petroleum products from wellhead to customer. The Federal Trade

Commission, taking the U.S. government point of view that competition is good and monopoly is bad, instituted steps to break up the oil companies. In the meantime, Congress, under pressure from environmentalists, adopted their point of view that what is good for business is not necessarily good for the environment and passed the National Environmental Policy Act. The act placed on government the burden of proof that any major government action would not significantly harm the environment. (Environmentalists used the act in 1977 to abort the sale of Atlantic offshore oil leases to the major oil companies because their environmental impact statements were inadequate.)

Let's pause for a moment and consider which if any of the above actions could be considered creative and why. By the use of point of view and changing levels there were at least four, possibly five, creative new solutions. First, the oil companies enlarged their point of view and operated on new levels of structure, order and relation—the integrated oil company. The FTC, considering only its point of view, the literal requirements of its office, limited the new levels of structure, order and relation of the oil industry. The environmentalists changed their point of view from nature lovers to nature preservers and put effective pressure on government. To be fair, we must concede that Congress was creative. It adopted the point of view of the environmentalists and created a new structure, order and relation between government and business—the National Environmental Policy Act. Probably the environmentalists should again get credit for creatively applying the new law to the well-established practice of offshore drilling for oil.

An ironic development took place in 1977. The oil companies came up with another creative idea. *They adopted the point of view of the environmentalists.* The argued that breaking up the oil companies would have a significant adverse environmental impact, including "unnecessary depletion of our nation's natural resources" and possible new pollution from increased fuel consumption to transport petroleum products to rival companies. A federal judge ruled that the FTC would have to come up with a full environmental statement and might even have to correct its perspective: "In the rare case where the FTC determines that the severity of the offense does not justify the environmental cost of remedying it, no doubt we would all be better off bearing the anticompetitive effects rather than paying for competition without natural resources."

Of course it could be argued that the oil companies only gained time. But that was enough as the oil shortage of 1979 proved. Time is order and order is change, and another creative solution at a later time is always possible.

This is an example of how creative new solutions affect your life even though you might choose to ignore them. Would you prefer to be a passive witness to the creative efforts of others? Or would you rather participate in life's changing structures, orders, relations, levels and points of view? If you choose the latter, the world you create will be more your own.

EXERCISES

Kaleidoscope Nature of Our Experience

We are able to keep track of no more than three things at the same time. We generally are able to keep track of structure, order and relation at least to some degree, but adding a fourth and fifth element—levels and point of view—complicates the problem enormously. Therefore, many times we are forced to use only our own point of view and seldom venture off the level of our personal perception of "reality."

Kaleidoscopes and Teleidoscopes

In the case of both these instruments, the Greeks had *three* words for it. They share *eidos* (form) and *scope* (instrument for reviewing). *Kalos* is Greek for "beautiful" and *tele* for "far off." Both have structure, relation, order and an unvarying point of view (the viewer's own). Levels differ, however: the kaleidoscope's "beautiful forms" are internal; the teleidoscope's "far-off forms" are, of course, external.

Consider various ways the teleidoscope extends the kaleidoscope. Classify each way as a thinking skill: structure, order, relation, point of view and level.

The "F" Test

This test seems simple on the surface. All you have to do is count the number of f's in the following paragraphs. Results may vary because of:

1) Order—we tend to see what we want to see.
2) Relation—we tend to see what suits our purposes at the time.
3) Structure—we tend to see what our background has prepared us to see.

Now count the number of f's in the paragraph, reading it through only once, and record your total.

How Good an Inspector Are You?

Go through once and count the f's.

The necessity of training farmhands for first class farms in the fatherly handling of farm livestock is foremost in the minds of farm owners. Since the forefathers of the farm owners trained the farmhands for first class farms in the fatherly handling of farm livestock, the farm owners feel they should carry on with the family tradition of training farmhands of first class farms in the fatherly handling of farm livestock because they believe it is the basis of good fundamental farm management.

Total number of f's———

Answer:

We tend to overlook the "f" in the word "of." There are thirty six "f's."

II

Understanding Skills in Using Similarity, Difference and Change

Creativity is the result
of using learned characteristics.

Gerard Nierenberg

4

The Meaning and Operation of Order, Structure and Relation

Where order in variety we see,
And where, though all things differ, all agree.
　　　　　　　　　—Alexander Pope, *Windsor Forest* 1.11

The first three basic skills of creative thinking may now be considered in greater depth. They do not follow a set sequence and are used interchangeably throughout the book to emphasize this characteristic. Later, the fourth and fifth skills, changing levels and points of view, will also be analyzed at length. As adults, we must be reeducated by reexperiencing our thinking skills of knowing and using structure (difference), order (change) and relation (similarity). We see how structure, order and relation depend upon each other for definition. Watching how they operate in the world, we further understand how the performance of each is also dependent upon the others. Let us apply some of the concepts of structure, order and relation to our understanding of ordinary objects about us. Look at your right bare foot. What do you see? For one thing you see five toes. Toes are *structures*. Other *structures* are the ball, the arch, and the heel. When you put these *structures* in an *ordered relation*, they make on a higher level a *structure:* the foot. To be a foot, the toes should be attached to the ball, not the heel, because this would change the *relation* and then it would not be a foot. A specific kind of *relation* and *order* must occur to be a *structure*. The place of the middle toe is in the middle. The place of the big one is on the side. We then understand and have knowledge, the *structure* is a foot because the things appear *related* (similar), as judged by your past experience (order passed in time). If any of the above *structures, orders,* or *relations* sufficiently change, we would not know the resultant *structure* as a foot.

Consider ways we view a river. Think how the interaction of *relation* and *order* make up the unique *structure*—that river. First, the interplay between the water and the bed: the water carves its bed, the bed controls the water. They form a *relation*. Then the flow of water, changing in time and space, is the *order*. Each, the water, bed and flow, cannot be considered separately or even as independent segments of knowledge. If the water overflowed its banks or dried up, how would the *structure* "river" be affected? We would still know it as "that river." Winston Churchill understood this interplay when he was opposed to the plan to change and enlarge the House of Commons wrecked in bombing raids during World War II. He warned, "We shape our buildings and they shape us."

Let us examine the three skills—order, structure and relation—on some of the numerous levels of our understanding for an even greater appreciation of their usefulness.

ORDER

For the world was built in order and the atoms march in tune; Rhyme the pipe and Time the Warder, the sun obeys them, and the moon.
—Ralph Waldo Emerson, *Monadnock* st. 12

Understanding the Term "Order"

Order deals with *change* in time and space (growth, transformation, development, evolution). We discover order in response to such questions as: "What is the sequence, stage and cycle?" i.e., yearly cycle of earth around sun (at one level); "What are its sequences, stages and cycles?" i.e., daily revolutions of the earth on its axis (at a lower level). Order is involved with time/space, before/after.

In the creative thinking process we can utilize the skill of *ordering* on different levels when we think and use the following words, phrases and additional questions:

What are the phases and steps? Enlarge, reduce, speed up, slow down, distort, affect, rotate, direct, evolve.

Can it be expanded? Added to in time and space, repeated, intensified, ingredients increased, thickened, built up.

Can it be diminished? Condensed in time and place, shortened, lessened, limited, frequencies increased, eliminated, lightened.

Can it be reconstituted? Changed in time, boiled, frozen, softened, symbolized, abstracted, taken apart.

What are the interactions? Internalized—cause and effect.

What are the interworkings? Externalized—before and after.

Is sensory awareness present? Sight, hearing, sense of smell, sense of taste, sense of balance, awareness of pressure, temperature, muscle tone (awareness through change—which is order).

Alfred Korzybski, founder of the study of General Semantics, observes in *Science and Sanity:* "Order seems neurologically simpler and more fundamental than relation. It is a characteristic of the empirical world which we recognize directly by our lower nervous centers ('senses'), and with which we can deal with great accuracy by our higher nervous centers ('thinking'). This term seems most distinctly of the organism-as-a-whole character, applicable both to the activities of the higher, as well as lower, nervous centers, and so *structurally* it must be fundamental." He states that order is first in our experience.

Possibly the first sensation we are aware of is the ordered beating of our mother's heart while we are still in the womb.

Certainly among the first are our own rhythmic heartbeats and breathing, both of which we can hear and feel. We also become aware of visual rhythm—perceiving bit by bit the curve of the mother's eye, her nipple and breast. The distance at which infants see best is nine to twelve inches, the same distance between the mother's and infant's eyes when the mother is holding her baby. Thus we encounter rhythmic change, a basic feature of all life, in our earliest moments of living. In later life, however, when we create music or poetry, for example, at a more involved higher level, rhythm is no longer just our own beat; it can now be shared and expanded. In poetry, on still another level, a sonnet has an ordered structure made up of related elements such as accent, meter and rhyme which contribute to a measured flow of words in time—another definition of rhythm.

Henri Poincaré states: "A mathematical demonstration is not a simple juxtaposition of syllogisms, it is syllogisms *placed in a certain order,* and the order in which these elements are placed is much more important than the elements themselves."

Philip Jackson and Samuel Messick point out in the *Journal of Personality:*

> An assortment of debris gathered in a junkyard and the ordered arrangement of the same material by an artist serves to illustrate the distinction being made here. Any meaning derived from the random assortment of junk is fortuitous and is obtained either from a chance association between the elements or from irrelevant associations that the material might stimulate in the viewer. By contrast the ordered arrangement, if it is worthy of artistic notice, contains more meaning than can be understood at first glance. The color and shape of the objects, their texture, their spatial location, and their original function all combine to enhance their aesthetic appeal.

STRUCTURE

Understanding the Term "Structure"

Structure deals with *differences* (contrasts, distinctions) and responds to questions such as: "What is the separate category, generalization, aggregate, dimension, and distinction?" e.g., the differentiation from others, living—nonliving (at one level). "What are its separate categories, generalizations, aggregates, dimensions, and distinctions?" e.g., the differences within dogs, cats, and cows (at a lower level).

In the creative thinking process we can utilize the skill of *structuring* on different levels when we think and use the following words, phrases and additional questions:

Can it be adapted? What is it similar to? Does it copy anything else? What is it like? What is this a kind of? What are its kinds? What does it do? What is it for?

Can it be sorted separately? What is its character? What is its property? What is its kind? What is its type?

Does it have logical sensory and/or emotional qualifications? What is its substance? What is its shape? What is its size? What is its number? What is its effect on sensations? What is its effect on the emotions?

We attempt to crystallize an ever-changing world and we do this by making structures. Korzybski says: "In structure we find means by which the event can always be made intelligible to us and so properly evaluated." And further in circular definition: "Structure can be considered as a complex of relations and ultimately as multi-dimensional order."

As order deals with time and space, structure tends to be timeless. To grasp the concept of the atom, for example, we may freeze it at a particular moment in time and thus are able to "see" the structure. We think we hear a melody, but actually we hear only one note of it at a time. Memory and, to some degree, anticipation, structure the individual notes into what we term "melody." The order ("timing") of the related parts (notes) provides higher structures (dimensions) to round out the conceptualization of a still higher structure (melody).

Our ability to "see" structures (differences) on many levels, from the subatomic to the universal, and in many modes—verbal, sensory, abstract and so forth—influences the way we respond to reality, our outside world. When we consider structure as "timelessness," we tend to make our thoughts and action about it somewhat inflexible and unchanging. Some feel it would be difficult to wake up each day to a completely restructured world (although we know intellectually that that is precisely what has happened). So their cumulative structures tend to resemble a family photograph album—fixed in time (except that the edges may curl and brown with age) of a past reality.

We are capable of transforming our structures into opposite, contrary, competing structures on different levels. For example, one of the most enduring structures in American life is the lapel button trumpeting many transitory causes. So, in keeping with tradition, the Consumer Product Safety Commission ordered 80,000 buttons promoting toy safety. Someone apparently decided to look below the surface of the structure and found the buttons had sharp edges that could cut, paint with too much lead in it, and clips that could be broken off and swallowed by small children. The buttons were recalled. Who would think that the structures (buttons) designed to promote safety would prove to be harmful on another level?

RELATION

Understanding the Term "Relation"

Relation deals with *similarities* (connections, affiliations) and responds to such questions as: "What is it a class of, what is it a part of, and what has it a connection with?" i.e., the genus—organism (at one level). "What are its classes, parts, and connections?" i.e., its members, plants and animals (at a lower level).

In the creative thinking process we can utilize the skill of *relating* on different levels when we think and use the following words, phrases and additional questions:

Can it be reversed? What about the opposites? Try reversals in different directions. Turn it inside out or upside down.

Can it be rearranged? What is it part of? What are the unit parts, separations? Can any pattern or layout be varied? Can transpositions be made?

What are the combinations? What are the integrated units of things, in time? What are its parts? Are there several purposes involved? Can it be divided? Multiplied?

What are alternatives? What can be substituted? Other parts, substances, times?

Can it be modified? What can be changed? Meaning, purpose, use, objective?

What are the similar qualifications? Is it an emotional state, possibly love, happiness, wonder, anger, terror, grief, or beauty?

Gaston Bachelard, the French philosopher, wrote: "As soon as even two properties of an object are known, they immediately get to be related. More advanced knowledge begets an exuberant growth of coordinated reasoning." The most basic types of relations are comparisons of similarities in any sort of connection.

If you had a rubber glove factory, could you manufacture a pair of rubber gloves with only a mold for a single hand? Yes, by turning one inside out and provided you made sure the inside and outside were of the same quality. When you want to fully consider the numerous types of relations available to you, check through the following examples:

In space, simple reversal can take place in many ways: (1) right to left, (2) top to bottom, (3) front to back, (4) inside out. (See Figure 3.)

In the world of the verbal and logical there are many more relational classifications for us to discover. For example, do we know when things are symmetrical, nonsymmetrical, and asymmetrical, transitive, nontransitive and intransitive?

Although relations are most clearly perceived on the intellectual level, the emotions often play a very active part in choosing the relationships we care to acknowledge. To a small child "mommy" is *his* mother and no one else's. It is only later, at the age of about three years, that he can from a higher level see that his playmates and even their mothers have "mommies" too. The relationship is no longer one-to-one but has become universal.

Relationship, colored by the emotions, is sometimes found to be unstable. A child may say, "I hate you!" one minute and "I love you!" the next. Psychiatrists call this ambivalence. The relationships remain on the same level and have not really changed. Only the emotional point of view has varied. Similarly, in music, much of the effect depends upon the ebb and flow of tension and repose (order) and the relationships between them. The ambiguities of relationships create many problems for people who have a deep need for a fixed order and a rigid point of view. Instinctively they know that both can be destroyed by shifting relationships. Thus they try to seal themselves off from change by making unreasonable demands that others "conform." That often irritating question, "Will you always love me?" is one such attempt. They do not seem to realize that the repeated question and the answer themselves can sometimes drastically alter the relationship.

Some people find it difficult to see new relations on different levels. Take, for example, this quotation by astronaut James Lovell, which appears in "The Liberated Woman's Appointment Calendar": "Well, we've never sent any women into space because we haven't had a good reason to. We fully envision, however, that in the near future we will fly women into space and use them the same way we use them on earth—for the same purpose."

William W. Sunderlin, an administrator of Westmoreland

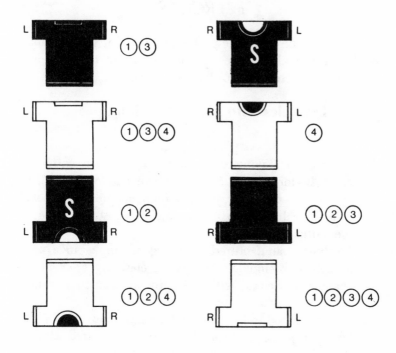

Figure 3

County, Virginia, adopted a point of view at a high level. He got tired of answering the Census Bureau's requests for information that always began, "Dear Friend." He knew he was "talking" with a computer, not another human being. So in the space marked "Comments" he wrote, "I'm your slave—not your friend." His perception of the relationship was confirmed almost at once. "Dear Slave," the letter began. "Thank you for your response."

EXERCISES

In examining the following problems, endeavor to look separately for the alternative approaches under the thinking skills of (S) structure, (O) order and (R) relation.

Examples with Alternative Solutions

1. Methods of making a smoking pipe which is easier to clean: R—forced smoke or bag smoke; bag for smoke like exhaust; R—no smoke, just sensation, acupuncture spots; S—replaceable bowl; O—no smoking—just go through the motions.

2. Clothing manufactured cheap, good appearance and durability: R—molded, body (skin), elasticity; O—control changing styles (as with Asian Indian women wearing saris); S—copy space suits.

3. Cheap method to indicate for typists the lowest possible line of type on a sheet of paper: S—measured plastic strip; S—zero meter show bottom; R—mirror to show bottom; O—roller on typewriter stops at end.

4. Simple methods for measuring flow of materials through pipes: S,O,R—pressure clock specifying gravity.

5. Methods to peel onions without causing eyes to burn: S—glasses, goggles, clench match or toothpick between teeth, or breathe through mouth rather than nose; O—behind back; R—spouse.

6. Methods for keeping surfaces such as billiard tables level: S—legs like hydraulic brakes; O—leveling procedure to set legs; S—float on sea of small ball bearings; R—use gyroscopes and pumps to level.

7. New methods for keeping up knee-length stockings: S—sock stays, spiral stays of air; O—walking fills air; R—air curled sock.

EXAMPLE

Problems for Creative Thinking

1. Methods for building roads that will cut maintenance costs.

   Structure: (a) Use more durable materials
                (b) Confine vehicles to a track
                (c) Increase width of tires—road maintenance lowered—use money elsewhere

   Order: Enforce antilitter laws by collecting fines

   Relation: (a) Ban heavy trucks
               (b) Limit uses
               (c) Grade road same as terrain

2. Methods to absorb sound.

   Structure: (a) Create a surrounding vacuum
                (b) Use acoustical materials
                (c) Use earmuffs to baffle sound

   Order: (a) Change frequency
               (b) Change volume

   Relation: (a) Overlay sound on sound (ocean wave sounds, etc.)
               (b) Desensitize by distracting sensory disguise
               (c) Desensitize by prolonged exposure to anesthesia

3. Dictating letters without a stenographer.

   Structure: (a) Write in longhand
                (b) Machine—speak into and print

   Order: (a) Recorder or telephone
               (b) Extrasensory perception

Relation: (a) Any other person not called stenographer

                 (b) Send recorded tape

4. Controlling ocean tides for energy.

Structure: Build dam with pipe

Order: Rising and falling creates energy

Relation: Long low flat dam which rising tide overrides, then flows back to sea through a generator.

5. New methods of filing papers cheaply and more efficiently.

Structure: Microfilm, video, microfiche

Order: Develop good retrieval system

Relation: (a) Cheaper labor

                 (b) Separate files for each person

6. Method to keep a room automatically ventilated.

Structure: (a) Holes in walls

                 (b) Fans

Order: Change room—no walls

Relation: (a) Rotate room

                 (b) Ventilate people

7. Simple method to fasten pages together in book form.

Structure: (a) Mechanical clamps

                 (b) Magnetize papers

                 (c) Glue that doesn't dry completely

Order: Have all on one continual page

Relation: Drill hole—finger holds it

8. A means of preventing rugs from rolling up at the corners and making them trip-proof.

Structure: (a) Heavier weave
                    (b) Change idea of rug—metal
                    (c) Wall-to-wall rug
                    (d) No doors in room
                    (e) Take off floor
Order: Project a picture of a rug on the floor.
Relation: Proper fit and installation.

Applications of the Thinking Skill of Order

1. Every experience is an opportunity to practice our skills. While sitting across from fellow passengers in a bus or train, look them over. How did that man look as a one-month-old infant? How did that girl look this morning when she awakened? How will the five-year-old boy look at fifty? How did that fifty-year-old man look at five? This is an experiment in change (order). By forcing yourself to imagine change, you become more skillful in handling it.

2. a) Find a series of pictures, each of which is in process—that is, changing in time and place. Write out as many causes as you can think of or what action is occurring in the pictures shown. You can use the events and things that have happened just before the event in the picture or even something that has happened a long time prior to the event. Give as many observations as you can.

   b) List as many possibilities as you can of what will be the consequences that take place after the events depicted in a front-page newspaper picture, either immediately after or a long time in the future. Make as many observations as you can.

Tests for Recognizing the Use of Structure, Order and Relation

Question 1: A man has 25 used cigar butts. It takes him

5 butts to make a cigar. How many cigars can he smoke after he has made them? (Hint: look for structures.)

Question 2: How many grooves does the ordinary 12-inch, 33⅓RPM phonograph record have? (Do you see them as different or similar? Hint: look for order.)

Question 3: If there were two horses in a race and you were concerned that the jockey was influenced by someone, in what way could you make sure that by having complete control of the race there would be an honest race? (Hint: look for relations.)

Answers to the above questions:
1. Six. Five from the original 25 butts and one more from the leftover butts from the five (seeing structure).
2. Two. One on each side (seeing order).
3. Have each jockey ride the other's horse (seeing relation).

Which thinking skills will help solve the following problems?

Applications of the Thinking Skill of Relation (Similarity)

Problem A: What is the area of the square in Figure 4a?

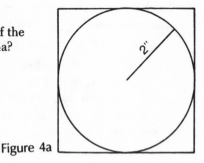

Figure 4a

Answer:

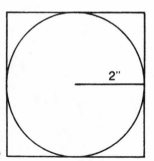

Consider relation. Change to relation shown in Figure 4b which makes it easier to visualize.

Figure 4b

Problem B: In the following series of numbers 1, 12, 1, 1, 1, 2, 1, 3, what are the next four numbers? (Answer is arrived at by considering order and relation.)

Considering order alone does not supply the answer. However, when order and relation are jointly thought of, the answer comes more quickly. You can consider order and relation when you ask yourself, "Where could I find a series?" The answer is on the face of a clock.

Answer: The numbers are 1, 4, 1, 5.

ORDER

A.   What time does the clock show? How many additional things can be added to show time?

B.   Is it A.M. or P.M.?

C.   What difficulties do you have reading the time?

D.   What systems does the clock measure?

E.   In what ways can the time indicated on a clock be changed? (Consider structure, order and relation.)

F.   Consider additional ways of measuring time.

STRUCTURE

Add lines to make recognizable objects from the forms below.

Use structure, order, relation, level and point of view.

STRUCTURE: SAME BUT DIFFERENT

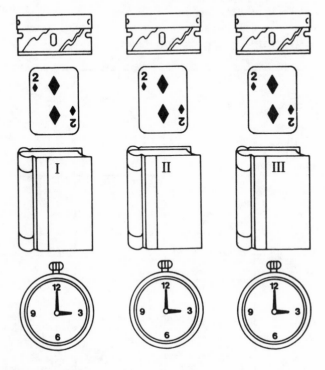

1. List similarities of items in each row.
2. List differences of items in each row.

STRUCTURES CHANGE

List as many uses for a penny nail as you can think of in five minutes.

_____

_____

_____

_____

_____

_____

_____

_____

_____

RELATION

Factors Used in Considering Relation

In the following list are some of the factors we use to consider relation.

1. Sensory
2. Similarity
3. Part-to-whole
4. Abstraction
5. Whole-to-part
6. Logic
7. Classes
8. Analogy

Can you enlarge the uses of penny nails considering any of the above?

Mirror Images—Changes Relation

Hold a mirror at the top, bottom and both sides of the letters shown below—letters having special mirror images. Look at the reflected images. Notice how, in some positions they change, others they do not. Can you find a special relation that holds true for the mirror image "S" by holding the mirror in one position and revolving the page?

C H O I C E

B   C   D   E   H   I   K   O   X

HEX   BIDE   EXCEED   DECODE

A   H   I   M   T   U   V   W   X   Y

TOOT   MOM   TUT   MUM   OTTO

A List of Terms Used in Logic for Relations

1. Transitive symmetrical   "being as young as"

2. Transitive asymmetrical   "forebears of"

3. Transitive nonsymmetrical   "not younger than"

4. Intransitive symmetrical   "spouse of"

5. Intransitive asymmetrical   "mother of"

6. Intransitive nonsymmetrical   "nearest living heir of"

7. Nontransitive symmetrical   "cousin of"

8. Nontransitive asymmetrical   "employee of"

9. Nontransitive nonsymmetrical   "friend of"

How Many Relations Can you Discover?

_____

_____

_____

_____

_____

5

General Semantics: Additional Uses of Structure, Order and Relation

. . . no man is complete, unless he consciously realizes the permanent presence in his life of some standards of evaluation. Everyone has thus some epistemology.
—Alfred Korzybski, *Science and Sanity*

A study of general semantics can provide one with methods of evaluating other methods of *evaluation*. In so doing it has recognized the importance of the terms order, structure and relation. We start with order because it is considered in general semantics the more basic term.

First, the term *order* is used as a concept to deal with the scientifically accepted premise that we are living in a "process" world with everything constantly in change at varying rates of speed. Our ability to set criteria in any method to deal with this process world is aided by our ability to understand order.

Second, the term *structure* implies that everything in the world that we view is unique and different. No two things examined in great detail are exactly the same. Complete sameness between any two things has never been demonstrated. We should always be aware of difference in any method. Uniqueness and nonidentity of all things are to be recognized as commonplace.

Third, the term *relation* implies that, in spite of the basic understanding of differences, we use the skill of relation to observe and respond as well to similarities. Without our ability to deal with the past by making relations, we would have neither memory nor intelligence. Every method must allow for this.

Human beings are conscious of similarities and differences as well as change. These concepts apply to all of the world around us—all methods and systems. They are a type of blueprint, which we have somewhat blindly followed from the moment of birth in dealing with the outside world. Our lives could be richer creatively if we used the time to appreciate and discover differences, similarities and change.

Experiments and demonstrations of general semantics use of creative thinking terms:

Structure

1. *Nine Dots Experiment.* Nine dots are arranged in a boxlike pattern. Draw four continuous connected straight lines through the nine dots. (See Figure 5 for solution.)

Most people tend to be frozen into the boxlike pattern. When they stop thinking of boxes and think of the problem, connecting nine separate dots, the solution opens up. Even three, two or one line can connect all of the dots. (See Figure 5a and b for answers.)

The problem becomes more interesting and requires additional thought if you are asked to connect all nine dots with *one* continuous line. It is possible to do if you think in a barrier-breaking, non-Euclidean way and break away from the flat surface. Make a cone out of the paper and draw a continuous line around the inside or outside connecting the dots. (See Figure 5c for answers.)

2. *The Dime Experiment.* You are given a U.S. dime and a card with a hole one-quarter inch in diameter that is smaller in diameter than the dime. The problem is to push the dime through the hole. If you only pay attention to self-imposed structural boundaries it becomes impossible. You close your mind to solutions such as to nudge the dime with a pencil struck through the hole, or to grind up the dime.

3. *The Three- by Five-Inch Card Experiment.* A group of people are asked to measure a three- by five-inch card and write the measurements on the card. Surprisingly, the results are not the same. We are instructed to consider instruments for measuring as absolutes rather than objects with the same structural limitations and differences as any other worldly thing.

4. *IX Demonstrations.* You are asked to add a line to IX to make a six. If you have difficulties, think of how you are thinking of a six: as a Roman numeral, as an Arabic numeral, or as a word. If it is in the last system, the solution becomes obvious: SIX.

5. *Taste Test.* If you ask different people to describe the taste of an experimental material, you will get different responses. However, people who are related tend to taste the same flavor. Thus the structure of our taste sensations is influenced in part by heredity.

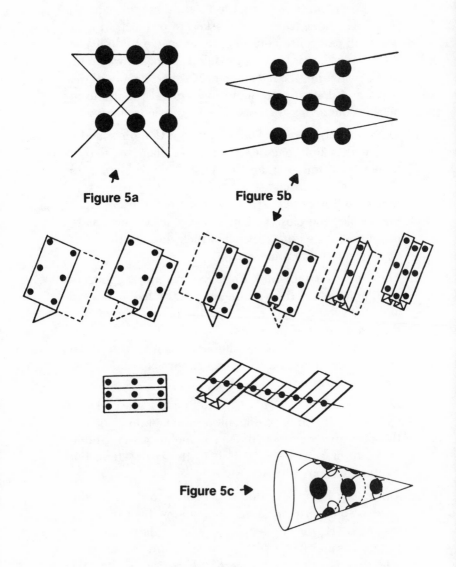

Figure 5a

Figure 5b

Figure 5c ➡

Figure 5

What have we changed in using structure, order, relation, level and point of view to obtain additional solutions?

RELATION

1. *The Three-Can Demonstration.* Take three one-pound coffee cans. Fill one with lead weights, one with sand, and leave one empty. Ask another person to lift the cans one after the other. Each lifting will produce a response of uncertainty and surprise: the lead and the sand because of different expectations, and the empty one because the person expects to be surprised.

2. *The Cone Demonstrations.* When an object that looks like two three-inch ice cream cones placed mouth to mouth is put on the middle of slightly inclined tracks which meet at one end and are three inches apart at the other end, the object rolls *up* rather than *down* the inclination. We tend to think that all objects only obey the law of gravity. We forget the relation of an object and a surface: for example, a ball and an inclined plane versus a cone and an inclined plane can behave differently.

3. *The Coin Demonstration.* At a certain age children relate size with "more." Therefore, the child would quite "logically" choose a half dollar rather than an old twenty-dollar gold piece.

ORDER

1. *The Bird-Song Demonstration.* If you play recorded bird songs at one quarter the normal speed, you will note many details that you had been unaware of. We unconsciously realize the relation between speed and comprehension when we slow our own speech while talking to a foreigner (or even worse, raise our voice).

2. *Probability Demonstration.* By using the bell-shaped curve to predict probability, we can predict more accu-

rately the percentage performance of 240 balls in a pin-ball machine than we can the course of a single ball.

3. *Knot-Tying Demonstration.* Ask a boy scout to tell you how to tie a Spanish Bowline, while you try to duplicate the motions with your hands behind your back. Do not be surprised if you agree with the man trying to give directions: you can't get there starting from here.

6

Increase Positive Results by Interchanging Structure, Order and Relation

Some men see things as they are and ask, "Why?" I see them as they have never been and ask, "Why not?"
—George Bernard Shaw

Although we use our notions about the terms structure, order and relation interrelatedly at all times, the ability to separate each concept intellectually can assist us creatively. There are occasions when we can expand our creative thinking ability by intentionally interchanging one creative thinking skill for the other two, or two for the three. We can then use the altered thinking patterns to examine the problem in advance of its actual occurrence and gain new working knowledge. We can substitute the skill of structure and relation for order and sometimes we can substitute order for structure and relation.

An example of this involves a driver in a moving automobile. His situation is constantly changing. As time passes, his location changes. He recognizes on a macrovisual level that his state is constantly changing. As he looks ahead he sees other cars in relation to him constantly changing. The cars are moving along the highway to the distant horizon. If he thinks creatively, the fact that when his *structure* (car) reaches the distant point of the highway, the *relations* (conditions) that those other cars are *now* experiencing will be the experience that he *will be* having in a short time. He sees a possible *order* before it happens. He therefore in essence looks into a future time frame. With this realization of order, many people change lanes, noting that far ahead one lane is moving faster than another. They anticipate that it will be advantageous for them to move into the faster lane.

Many drivers will not look, some will not see, a few, not knowing how to use the information laid out in front of them, will change (order) into the next lane (structure) because it is moving faster (relation) at present. They may end up in a slower lane or even have an accident.

Is it possible for us to use our creative thinking skills to see "into the future" in other situations? That is the intent in problem solving. To illustrate, this problem could be approached by hypothetically interchanging structure, order and relation. If a commercial laundry possessed ten trucks, how could it best route these trucks through the service area? The objective would be to cover a certain number of stops at the smallest cost and the least time. This is a problem in which the number of trucks, area, timing, stops and change of place are all translatable into the thinking skills of structure, order and relation. You will appreciate how each is part of the other. Possible solutions include:

Structure: Increase or decrease the number of drivers, trucks or stops.

Relation: Change direction of paths of travel or interchange truck stops. Interchange drivers.

Order: Change sequence of stops. Start and stop at different times. Consider time of day and seasons.

Because of the large number of variables, computers have been most helpful in making alternatives available.

As can be said of the laundry business: "A cleaner look at the future makes a brighter one."

STRUCTURE, ORDER, RELATION LEVELS AND POINT OF VIEW AS MEMORY AIDS

1. Relation
    1. Rhymes
    2. Spacial arrangements
    3. Alphabetizing
    4. Chain-link—related to each other
    5. Scheduling—related to time

2. Structure
    1. Key words
    2. Images
    3. Mobile/immobile
    4. Discover cues

3. Order
    1. Timing
    2. Stimulate interest
    3. Look from past to future
    4. Construct patterns—repeatable

4. Level
    1. Whole-to-part more useful than part-to-whole
    2. Use different senses—see and hear
    3. Use different skills—write, read, recite

The following symbols use Structure, Order and Relation. Change Level to See an Entire System

⌐| = 1   ¬ = 2   ⌐ = 3

|_| = 4   □ = 5 |⌐ = 6

L = 7   [= 8   Γ = 9

X = 0

ANSWER:

9	6	3
8	5	2
7	4	1

5. Point of View
    1. Concentrate on important points
    2. Adapt to subject matter
    3. Intention to remember

Aristotle's System of Classification
As a Memory Aid

1. *Spacial,* e.g., floor plan
2. *Temporal,* e.g., three o'clock in the morning
3. *Similarity of class,* e.g., a dog, a cat
4. *Contrast,* e.g., whiter than white
5. *Causality,* e.g., Who put the overalls in Mrs. Murphy's chowder?
6. *Parts/whole,* e.g., "A fool there was and he made his prayer to a rag and a bone and a hank of hair."
7. *Number,* e.g., "How do I love thee? Let me count the ways."

7

The World of Levels Surrounds Us—Opens Creativity

The heavens themselves, the planets and this center
Observe degree, priority, and place,
Insisture, course, proportion, season, form,
Office and custom, in all line of order.
—Shakespeare, *Troilus and Cressida*
Act I, sc. 3, l. 85

The fourth creative thinking skill—changing levels—can be considered as a derivative skill because it results from utilizing the first three basic skills.

We all learn in the process of growing up that the world is made up of multiple levels. As adults, we have an endless array of hierarchies, arrangement in ranks or order, of the levels at which we think. We say that we may view objects or life from different levels such as submicroscopic, microscopic, macroscopic, telescopic, extratelescopic. We have organized life and classified all things in levels. As an example, human life could be organized to start at atomic level, then cellular, tissue, organ, body, family, clan, city, country.

When we change levels of viewing, for example, putting our naked eye to a telescope, appearances can change. Looking at what had appeared to be a single star might now be seen to be a cluster of two or more.

Whether we impose these hierarchies of levels on the things that we see around us or whether they even "exist" outside our minds is unimportant for our consideration. Probably we impose the hierarchies from the smallest to the largest or from the broadest to the narrowest because the thinking processes of "seeing" and classifying work hand-in-hand.

Consider the level in this example, if you place three dots thus:

Figure 6

You might view them as one-dimensional (three random dots), two-dimensional (isosceles triangle), or three-dimensional (a pyramid). On each abstraction level, structure, order and relation would appear to change and interchange. That which was considered order (sequence, three random dots) on one level may become structure (difference, pyramid) on another, into relation (similarity, isosceles triangle) on still another. The levels would also change if, instead of viewing the dots with the naked eye, we were to study them through a magnifying glass, a compound microscope and an electron microscope. Each would provide a different way of viewing and a lower level of abstraction. Our concepts of structure, order and relation would change. Figure 7 shows the way we hypothetically build our levels from our structures, orders and relations. One dot expands into a never-ending series of triangles. It grows more complex.

Each of our other senses can also change levels, amplify and diminish and alter our perceptual impressions of the concepts of structure, order and relation. We can even combine senses creatively. For example, John Randolph, in his description of a fellow politician united sight and smell to produce this: "He shines and stinks like rotten mackerel by moonlight."

The levels at which something can be better considered or evaluated reflects the kaleidoscopic nature of the impressions we perceive through our senses. The way that we apply

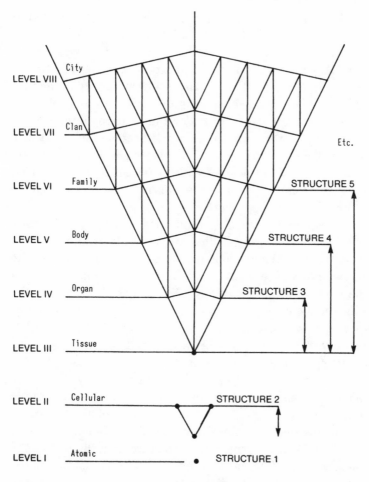

Figure 7

our concepts of them (point of view) give structure, order and relation.

At different levels our perceptions have or are given different characteristics. In abstracting, we tend to appreciate only one level and limit our considerations merely to the characteristics we are interested in. As an example, if a person felt ill, the limited characteristics we abstract would designate a level of treatment. If one were going to treat the mind, he might treat it with psychoanalysis. If he wanted to treat an organ or the body, he might treat it with surgery. If one wanted to treat a tissue, he might treat it with special diets. If one wanted to treat a group of cells, he might treat them with a chemical. Many times a treatment is not helpful because of confusion concerning the appropriate level.

In considering structure, order and relation on the level of a cell, only certain aspects of a cell become clear. We will find that those same aspects change when we move to another level and are dealing with tissue, organ or body. That is, what we can know at one level is not necessarily what we can know at another level.

Let us take this as an example: If I show you a dot on a piece of paper and say, "What are we really looking at?" you might reply, "We are looking at the light reflecting off the paper and we see a difference in the appearance between the white and black sections." You might also say, "By the way the light rays are undergoing a sequence of change (order), I see a black dot," or you might say, "I notice the relation of the black to the white, and because I see this relation and the difference in the order, I classify it as a structure, namely, a black dot." Then I might say, "Take the microscope and look at the black dot." Are you going to see it in the same way under the microscope? Not at all, because the microscope will now show you fibers, smudges, marks and globs. It is no longer the structure of a black dot. It's forestlike with different shadings and different carbon particles placed about. So, at the microscopic level below the ordinary macro viewing level, you see an entirely different set of structures, orders and relations. The structures are being broken down into the characteristic parts of their structure at lower levels. You will find that what you consider structure on one level now becomes relation of many structures. It is a forest of structures under the microscope.

Suppose you draw back from the dot and find it is not a single dot on the paper but is surrounded by other dots. Then you draw away from these other dots and find that these dots are of different shades and different colors. Moving further away, you suddenly find that the one dot you had been looking at is really part of the print of a picture. By bringing all of the other related dots into view you see it now on a macroscopic level as part of a photographic halftone section of the newspaper. So when you look at it now on a higher level, you say, "That's a picture." You do not see the dot any more.

This is what we do constantly by changing levels: the more views we have of the world the more we can become aware of our surroundings. But what we still fail to realize is the vast number of levels on which we operate. We also do not realize that we are constantly perceiving at different levels. We can only do this intellectually, because if we try to stop at one level it would be the same as if we were to stop the running of a motion picture. We know mentally that in the movie we are looking at a series of projected still frames, yet we have the ability to bring them all together intuitively and say we are looking at a "moving" picture.

In language we have symbolic levels. Some of the divisions are orders of meaning, description, inference, judgment and higher orders of abstractions. Even the symbolic levels we use can be limited by such things as our clichés. They often reveal our hidden assumptions about word meanings, freezing them at certain levels. One such is "overturning the established order," put into less rigid language by Tennyson. "The old order changeth, yielding place to new." The initial cliché implies a relatively limited meaning of a social or political structure that could only be replaced by revolutionary means. It betrays a reluctance to see any change in status quo other than by revolution. Tennyson, however, recognized the inevitability of change and avoided making a moral judgment on whether change is good or bad. His could be considered a broader view and therefore a higher level creative approach. At what level would this be? "It is in changing that things find repose" (Heraclitus).

The cultures we live in affect and add to our levels. Different concepts, of order, that is time and space and how we organize it are found in different societies. Societies that do not depend upon technology do not organize time elements (order) into the same levels that we do. The time units that lives are divided into are those to which one is required to respond. We have responded to the moving hands on our clock and now the seconds on our digital watches. An agricultural society will depend upon the seasons. The nomad will depend on available grazing land for his herds. When the fish return to spawn, when the birds nest, when the ice breaks up—these are things that mark the times of their lives. The same thing is true for levels of concepts of space. They differ as the culture dictates. It does not matter to an Eskimo the way an English language newspaper is held: upside down, right side up, or sideways. The direction of the writing is not important to him. He can "read" the letters any way they are placed, but he does not get the same cultural message on the level that we do. Natives of the jungle and children also share with the Eskimo the inability to see three dimensions in a two-dimensional photograph. When they have never seen a photograph they have difficulty visualizing. They will not even recognize a photo of their mother. It is culturally a learned skill to see at one level and conceptualize at another.

Understanding levels can also help us to see how we evolve moral hierarchies; further how they are useful to the different sciences to establish their hierarchies. We attempt to clarify our concepts of the outside objective world by starting with the more basic science levels such as physics and chemistry and then move on to biology and medicine. All of this will be discussed in later chapters.

From the countless levels and their hierarchies at our disposal, it is reasonably possible to find at least one that is applicable to a particular problem. By using the creative thinking skill of changing levels, you also change your point of view along with the structure, order and relation. At some level, hopefully, you will find a usable creative solution to your problem.

Try imagining a change of symbolic level and discover an answer.

Problem:	You dream you are on a sinking ship with your mother and father. You could only save one. What can you do?
An answer:	Wake up. (Dreaming is symbolizing.)
Problem:	Their is four errers in this sentence. Can you find them?
An answer:	Spelling: their and errers Grammar: is Change level: the fourth error is that there are only three errors in the sentence.

Using Figure 7 find a level that is most appropriate to place your problem used in the first exercise on page 83. By looking at the levels above and below your problem recognize the interrelationship and changeability of structure, order and relation.

8

Your Point of View—A Combined Creative Thinking Skill

Oh wad some power the giftie gie us
To see oursels as others see us!
It wad frae monie a blunder free us,
An' foolish notion.
        —Robert Burns, To a Louse

Every man is more than just himself; he also represents the unique, the very special and always significant and remarkable point at which the world's phenomena inter-sect, only one in this way and never again.
        —Hermann Hesse, prologue to *Demian*,
        trans. by Michael Roloff and Michael Lebeck

The fifth and final creative thinking skill, like changing levels, is also considered a derivative skill because it results from utilizing the other four skills. Our momentary point of view is the sum of the structure, order and relation and level at which we are participating.

Each and every person has a separate and distinct view of the world and understanding of what is going on. Sir Joseph John Thomson was awarded the Nobel Prize for establishing that electrons are particles. Thirty years later his son George Paget Thomson was also awarded the Nobel Prize when he proved electrons are waves. Both were right and are still right. Even scientific opposites (point of view) can both be "right."

As children we initially take the many impulses that come to us through our senses and give them a certain sequence, or *order*. In utilizing sequences in time, we see the color of a light or hear the musical tone of a note. The child also uses sequences in space, as in seeing the orderly arrangement of fingers on a hand, letters in a word and words on a page. Once a sequence is established, the mind almost at once imperceptibly shifts its focus to the *relation*, similarities, between the present ordered details and past experience. Then another shift is made. One mentally manufactures a *structure* that makes "sense" out of what are essentially unstructured, disordered and unrelated details. From all the vast ambiguous impulses coming into our senses from the world through our perceptions of structure, order, and relation and level, we construct our point of view of what is "out there." This does not mean that because of our individuality, we cannot achieve a "meaningful consensus" with others as to what is happening. This occurs most of the time. However, there will always be a slight and sometimes real difference between peoples' various points of view.

An interesting practice of the Sioux Indians helps them to understand point of view. When members of the tribe went outside their immediate area, they would offer this invocation: "Great Spirit, help me never to judge another until I have walked two weeks in his moccasins." Today, in a similar spirit, the U.S. Army does not promote officers to the rank of general unless they have had actual combat experience. It is felt that they would be more thoughtful about the risks, having been there.

Utilizing point of view is a creative thinking skill which can be extended when we intellectually master and consciously manipulate it. This is made possible by:

1. Seeing how use of relations has been limited to orientations based on our past experiences;

2. Broadening and making each experience more significant;

3. Understanding our orientation in the world;

4. Gaining insights outside our personal point of view, expanding alternatives available and appreciating the validity of other persons' points of view.

Let us consider each of these four items in detail.

1. Our mind tends to formulate our point of view to protect our preconceived ego. It even makes us distort, rationalize, or forget things. It sets up systems of logic and common sense which after a lifetime of devotion, on open examination, become shocking and contrary to new experiences. At first, it would seem impossible that anyone could break out of his unique point of view. How could we see the world except through our own eyes? Some simple experiments can help us illustrate this problem.

In an experiment in 1927, the Western Electric Company at the Hawthorne plant in Illinois, attempted to discover the effect of incentives on workers' production. At first, to their delight, as incentives were increased production went up. But, to their dismay, when incentives decreased production still climbed. This later became known as the "Hawthorne effect." Production increased when the workers were being made aware of what they were doing. Their point of view was changed, they were not just working but participating in a worthwhile experiment. Our point of view expands when we are involved in growth situations.

Some other similar psychological experiments that revealed insight into the limitation and expansion of one's point of view refer to the "halo effect" and "the observer affecting the observed."

For a personal experiment, return to an earlier discussion of the mirror (page 37). Look into the mirror and notice that in it letters appear backward but not upside down. Where you appear to have your right ear, the image has the left ear, and where you appear to have your left ear, the image has its right ear. You might say that this is an inversion. However, when you look at your forehead and chin, you find that there is no inversion vertically. What this seeming contradiction illustrates is that you are not looking at the mirror image but rather taking on the point of view of the mirror image so completely that you seemed to have changed the left and right orientation of parts of your body. *You* have become the eyes looking out of the image in the image looking at yourself and seeing behind you.° Many people are so used to seeing themselves in a mirror that they are not satisfied with and find unfamiliar an image of themselves that they see in a photograph. The image is not reversed, not their mirror image.

We are prepared to accept many things without question from our mirror image (our head at one fourth its size). On the bathroom mirror draw a line with soap around the outline of your face in the mirror. Move back and compare the circle you drew with the actual size of your face. When we perform a *familiar* action (shaving, putting on jewelry) using a mirror as a guide, we reverse our actions without question. Our point of view has changed. However, if we then try to use a mirror to guide us in an *unfamiliar* situation (e.g., attaching a screw in a spot we cannot see without a mirror) it takes time to adjust to the image of a new point of view.

Lewis Carroll in *Through the Looking Glass* showed more than passing interest in the peculiarities of mirror reflections, the reversal of many asymmetric relations. In the *London Times* for January 22, 1932, Alice Raikes, a distant cousin, tells how she played her own vivid part:

"One day, hearing my name, he (Charles Dodgson) called me to him saying, 'So you are another Alice. I'm very fond of

---

° To understand why no vertical inversion of the forehead and chin takes place in the mirror in front of you, consider, in looking at mirrors, there are six different types of mirror images. The reversals can take place in each of the three dimensions. The mirror in front and back is vertical to you and reverses everything in depth (front to back). If you put mirrors on the ceiling and floor, when you look up and down, the mirrors would be horizontal to you and reverse everything in the vertical plane—your feet will be where your head should be, and your chin will be where your forehead should be. The third dimension, along each side, will reverse you in width. In addition, all images reverse left to right. (See Figure 8.)

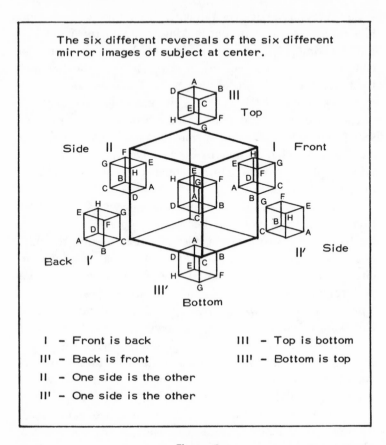

The six different reversals of the six different mirror images of subject at center.

III — Top

I — Front

II — Side

I' — Back

II' — Side

III' — Bottom

I — Front is back
II' — Back is front
II — One side is the other
II' — One side is the other

III — Top is bottom
III' — Bottom is top

Figure 8

Alices. Would you like to come and see something which is rather puzzling?' We followed him into his house which opened, as ours did, upon the garden, into a room full of furniture, with a tall mirror standing across one corner. 'Now,' he said, giving me an orange, 'first tell me which hand you have got that in.' 'The right,' I said. 'Now,' he said, 'go and stand before that glass and tell me which hand the little girl you see there has got it in.' After some perplexed contemplation, I said, 'the left hand.' 'Exactly,' he said, 'and how do you explain that?' I couldn't explain it, but seeing that some solution was expected, I ventured, 'If I was on the *other* side of the glass, wouldn't the orange still be in my right hand?' I can remember his laugh. 'Well done, little Alice,' he said. 'The best answer I've had yet.' "

Lewis Carroll in *Through the Looking Glass* went on to write about how all the actions of his characters would be on the other side of the glass.

Figure 9 explains two other things about the mirror image: if you spread your thumb and forefinger apart—say, about two inches—the space it corresponds to in the mirror image will remain constant in the mirror image no matter how close or how far you are from the mirror. Also, if you stand far back from a long, narrow mirror, the image will reflect the same amount of your body as it will when you stand close.

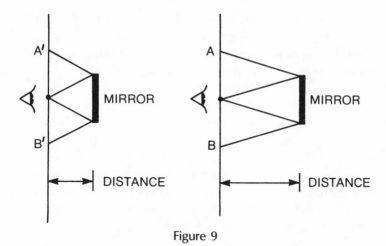

Figure 9

AB and A'B' always appear the same distance apart no matter what the distance between the mirror and the observer.

Without doing so, could you decide whether from a frontal point of view your signature would be reversed if you wrote it across the face of a mirror or on a plate glass one inch in front of a mirror?

As a final illustration of point of view and reversal of asymmetric relations: Put a thin cotton glove on your right hand, then put both hands together in the steepling position (a gesture that is made when you join your fingertips and form a "church steeple"). Now pull off the glove, turning it inside out, and transfer it from the right hand to the left hand. You have made a reverse image. All basic qualities of the glove hand have remained the same except point of view. We note the glove is inside out in reference to its last position. This shows point of view is to be considered a separate creative thinking skill because it can bring about a difference where the structure, order, relation and level of understanding seem to remain the same. What difference does it make to the glove to be inside out? The change is only within the observer.

2. All of the illustrations in the last section above also show how results of experience can limit us. With the creative thinking skills in mind, experience *now* can broaden our points of view and be made more useful.

3. One's orientation might be further amplified by considering that we each have our subjective world and there is a commonly understood and universally agreed-upon objective world. In the objective world, mirror images, upside down, left-right, inside out, intelligent-nonintelligent are all relative terms that do not change structure, order and relation. They all deal with orientation of the observer, and the observer is you, which is your point of view and your subjective world.

The following lines contain an exercise. After you read them, stop and do the exercise before going on.

Lie on your back on a horizontal surface. Lift your arms overhead. Now do it.

Were your arms *over your head* or did they point to the ceiling? Some of us do it one way, some the other. You can see that with merely a change in the orientation of your body position, your point of view can change. Our point of view and orientation are mutually dependent.

4. Finally, to open yourself up to insights, alternatives, and appreciation of points of view, start another experiment: When you awake in the morning, before you open your eyes, open just one eye and carefully observe all the things around you. Now close that eye and open the other eye. Carefully observe all the things that you see around you. You will notice that each eye gives you a different image of the outside world. When you open both eyes, if you have normal vision, you will get a binocular agreement of the world. We need two eyes to see "straight." As John Ross wrote in "The Resources of Binocular Perception," *Scientific American,* March 1976:

> Furthermore, when monocular perception conflicts with binocular constructs, the monocular percepts are suppressed.

The article continues, referring to his experiments and general conclusions:

> Square targets are more perfectly square, with more perfect edges than any real square. They are like the Platonic form of a square. What we observe in random dot-stereograms may well be idealized conceptions, imposed on the external flow of information by something within the visual system. What we observe may be a structure built by vision when it adjusts itself as it tunes in to the sources of information it can sense. Just as a computer has a program, so may the visual system have a program of arrangements for shapes in space and time. What we see is an interpretation of the external world, ordered within a framework the visual system imposes because of the attitude it adopts. In other words, we adopt a perceptual attitude in order to comprehend the world.

These conclusions would seem to illustrate that we impose our structures, orders and relations on the data received through our senses. This helps form our point of view. With the ability to change our point of view, we gain an awareness of what we have been doing and, further, what we can do.

Experiments have been conducted that seem to indicate that either side of the brain could perform most of the functions that are required by the body. Those who sustain injuries during their first year, where one side of the brain is rendered inactive, are able to relocalize functions and to carry on a fairly normal functioning life. However, if the injury occurs later in life, there is greater difficulty in rehabilitation, many times resulting in complete incapacity. It would appear that the brain is set up to function so that two separate points of view come together under some sort of agreement and the body performs pursuant to that agreement. Each side of the brain, capable of functioning independently, as is each eye, compares its impulses with those of the other side and an agreement is reached which in some instances may not even be in conformity with the outside world.

Illusion can be the name given to the compromise agreements that the brain reaches which have little basis in reality. On a fairly low level are the more than two hundred geometrical illusions that have been discovered and recorded. Some are shown in Figure 10. Like many "simple" things, although it is easy to explain what happens, no one seems in agreement on why it happens. One theory is that we view the two-dimensional drawings as three-dimensional scenes. The drawing in Figure 1 (see page 9) shows the distortions that can take place when we "guess" what the third dimension will be. (Interestingly, the misapprehension of geometrical illusions is most vivid at first glance. Apparently experience and changing points of view result in "disillusionment.")

On a higher level, Adalbert Ames, Jr. shows that the physical nature of things may differ from their appearance. One example is the trapezoidal window experiment: because in our culture we most often see only rectangular windows,

Figure 10

when a cardboard picture of a window shaped like a tra-
pezoid with one parallel edge shorter than the other is
mounted on a base motor and revolved slowly, rather than

objectively observing that the window is trapezoidal, the mind draws the erroneous conclusion that it is like "all" other windows and is rectangular. During the slow revolutions, when the short edge is at the rear or in the front, it creates the illusion that it appears to stay in the rear and swing back and forth like a ball on a string.

Another experiment is the distorted room. This consists of constructing a room according to strict perspective so that it looks like a normal room. When people are added, however, the distortion is obvious. But the people are distorted in size so that an adult in the furthest corner shrinks and seems smaller than a child up front. One theory is that our mind in conformity with experience, our mental set, "knows" the room is cubical. To be fully consistent, we conceive a distorted image of the people. There are still other Ames experiments—ways in which we see our subjective structure, order and relation rather than "actual" objects.

A different type of experiment is called the newspaper headline illusion. Someone stands with a newspaper just outside the limit of your clear vision. At this point you should not be able to read the headline. The person holding the paper then tells you what the headline is. Immediately the headline forms in your mind and you can then actually see it. Your expectation aids your ability to read. This allows us to understand that the act of seeing takes place in more than the eyes. We should realize that our point of view is malleable. It is made up of the same quality and substance as an illusion, not unchangeable absolutes.

How might we utilize the potential of the operations of parts of the brain if we were to consider it as similar to the operation of viewing a holographic medium? In the holographic picture, every part of the entire picture is contained in each part of the holographic medium. Possibly by shifting approaches to ideas through different parts, processes and sections of the brain, we can force a change of point of view and levels.

Some psychologists, in efforts to study creative problem

solving, have divided the problems into what they call personal factors and situational factors. This terminology would seem to indicate that structure, order and relation are personal factors (of the person). Points of view would be situational factors. Therefore, with an ability to expand our points of view, we could take in more of an experience (situation).

The following are some experiments with expanding situational factors. The Gestalt psychologists have been interested in the *influence* of the surrounding environments on problem-solving abilities. They have shown that if things necessary for the solution are in your visual field (point of view) of the procedure, the problem can be more easily solved. The German psychologist Wolfgang Köhler, one of the founders of Gestalt psychology, wrote the famous book, *The Mentality of Apes,* where he observed the same phenomenon in apes. A female ape was able to use a stick as a rake in order to pull food inside her cage. However, when the stick which she had used before was behind her, out of her field of vision, she did not consider its "instrumentation" of value when she was gazing directly at the food. Things necessary to solve the problem had to be within her field of vision in order to be made use of without hesitation.

When we understand other points of view, we are expanding our own point of view. When we expand our point of view, we gain additional alternatives.

Further illustrations are offered in the next chapter.

Exercises Using Point of View

1. Read a story. Examine it for different points of view. Look for any hidden points of view. In some stories a hidden point of view is the writer's. Try to change significance by changing point of view. Do we change values by changing point of view?

2. Consider a recent personal problem. Write your inter-

pretation of important points in the problem. If possible, get a similar interpretation of the problem from as many of the other involved parties as possible. Compare and see if their points of view agree.

3. You have a CHOICE with mirror images. There's not just one mirror image, there are six. In some instances the printing of this page will change, in other instances the words will remain the same. Can you explain the illusion?

    Put the mirror at the top of the page and read in the mirror the word CHOICE. Put it on the left side of the page, read the word CHOICE; put it on the right side of the page, read the word CHOICE; put the mirror at the bottom of the page, read the word CHOICE. Again, why is it in some instances the word CHOICE remains the same when the appearance of all other words on the page change?

4. Words made from the following printed letters do not appear to reverse in a mirror image:

    Mirror held at top or bottom of page: B, C, D, E, H, I, K, O, X, e.g., HEX, BIDE, EXCEED, DECODE.

    Mirror held at side of page: A, H, I, M, I, T, U, V, W, X, Y, e.g., TOOT, MOM, TUT, MUM, OTTO.

    For the fun of it, try to write a few sentences with hidden words which reveal a secret message through their mirror image.

5. It was known to the ancients that the moon appears bigger at the horizon than at its zenith. This is of course not the case, nor is it the effect of refraction. Use a ruler and measure the moon's diameter at its zenith and at the horizon. The diameters are exactly the same. The illusion appears to be the result of seeing the moon in reference to familiar objects on the horizon, in which event it appears bigger than at its zenith.

6. Look through a stereoptic viewer. You will see dimensions and depth. This is caused by a reversal of point of view. Instead of your eyes seeing two different images in relief and therefore signaling the brain that a single image is in relief, each picture image of the stereoptic viewer offers your eyes two plane images; they are however slightly different. They produce what your eyes would see if it were one single image in relief. The picture that is being sent to the brain is the same for the two plane images as it would be if you were looking at a single image in relief.

An important factor now becomes apparent in how our points of view change relationships. In Figure 3 (see page 57), in which a sweater is placed in different relationships, different apparent changes occur or do not occur. In placing the mirror to see six different mirror images, the letter S always appears backwards. The reason for this is that in all mirror images, left and right are reversed.

Now let us try a test in which we will reverse this page by turning it upside down 180° and notice the S still appears as an S. To compare this reversal to what occurs in Figure 3, if we were to imagine an S on the front of the sweater, the only other sweater on which the S would appear as a readable S would be the reversal of 1 (right to left) and 2 (top to bottom).

EXERCISE

The illusions can change with a change in point of view.
These drawings are outside our normal point of view.

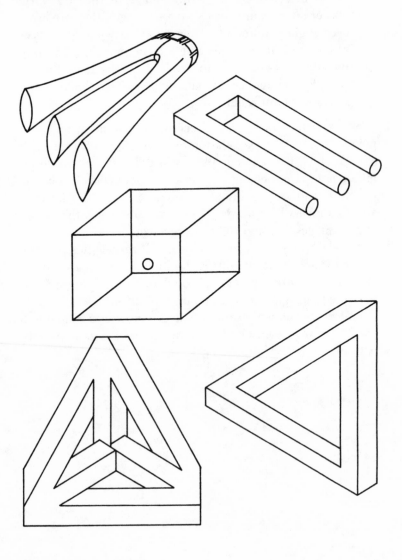

III

Additional Understanding of Your Other Mental Methods and Systems

Truth is what stands the test of experience.
Albert Einstein, *Out of My Later Years*

9

Change Thinking with Levels and Points of View

Far better never to think of investigating truth at all than to do so without a method.

—René Descartes

How have you tried to solve past problems that have required creative (new) solutions? Probably you did it with some form of accidental changing of structure, order, relation, point of view, or level, but with no conscious realization of what you were doing or intentional application of a combination of the creative thinking skills. We now understand this was normal, familiar and comfortable, but far from adequate. From now on it is helpful and important to view your problems intentionally with each of the creative thinking skills specifically in mind, then separately and in combination apply them.

For example, if you have a business problem, you might start looking for a creative alternative by adopting the point of view of a partner or associate. To the degree you are familiar with these views, the shift will be relatively easy. Through these views you will find that the order, structure and relation of elements of your problem have subtly changed. Is this enough to provide a creative solution? If so, fine. If not, go a step further. Envision the point of view of a less close associate, a supplier, perhaps, whose views are also relatively familiar to you.

Moving methodically, step by step, you can with practice

see the problem from the viewpoint of a competitor, a customer, a friend, a neighbor, a stranger, a foreigner, perhaps even a Martian. Somewhere along a never-ending path of views should be an acceptable creative solution. If not, try changing levels. You can change levels, traveling up or down from any point. If downward, you might minutely analyze the structure, order and relation of a component of your problem, as well as the many, outside contributing parts. This can change your comprehension (former view) of the whole problem. If upward, the problem will be placed in the ever-broadening context of your family, your community, your industry or profession, your nation, the world.

You can with equal skill combine approaches. Move on to another point of view and then switch to a further change of levels. Use of one or the other may depend on availability, personal preference or ability, but both are equally effective and essential in providing creative solutions.

Changing the point of view was essential to solving the riddle of the king who offered his only daughter's hand in marriage to the wisest man in his kingdom. Those who chose to participate in the competition were warned that if they did not answer the question asked them correctly they would be executed. Three wise suitors appeared and the following problem was presented: They would be put into a room without a mirror or reflecting surface. Each would have a black or white dot on his forehead. They were not permitted to speak with one another. They had to determine whether their dot was black or white. The only special instruction was that if someone saw two white dots, he must raise his hand. They were put into the room. All had black dots on their foreheads. After a short while, one of the suitors left the room and said he had a black dot. The king asked, "How do you know?"

STOP. Try to work out the problem. The solution rests completely on understanding point of view.

He said, "I saw two black dots. I asked myself, 'Do I have

a black or white dot?' I then took the point of view of the person to my right. If he saw a white dot on me as well as the black dot that we saw in common *and* if the person to my left was not raising his hand, the person to my right, being smart, would know immediately that he had a black dot and would have answered the question. Because he did not, he must also be looking at two black dots. That is how I figured it out."

To understand what goes on about us, we must develop the creative skills of changing our point of view hypothetically. Then we begin to see what is happening in the world from different perspectives. Not only can this give us new creative insights, it is useful in understanding and dealing with our many relationships.

As we have seen, a shift in our point of view can change our concept of the structure, order and relation. So can a change in levels. A creative adult can discover a thing, process or action possessing a particular structure, order and relation on one level but then, when viewing it differently, establish perhaps a totally new set of relation, order and structure on another level. Alfred Korzybski, in *Science and Sanity* explains how forms and meaning change on different levels: "The main characteristic of terms consists of the fact that on different levels of orders of abstraction they may have different meanings with the result that they have no general meanings, for their meanings are determined by the given context, which establishes the different orders of abstraction."

In simply changing a level, new insights into problems in many disciplines can be realized. Learning experiences are made easier by comparing our understanding of relation (similarities) at different times (order). We can also divide experiences involving a present sensory event into microsensory or the macrosensory levels. Then we can locate the specific level that we find necessary to be able to relate to a past particular experience.

The ability to learn the audio Morse Code illustrates the

problem involved. One forth to one third of the adult population finds the audio Morse Code quite difficult to learn. To save time and expense, tests were designed during World War II to train only potential candidates. An understanding of what ability was needed in auditory identification could have been helpful in expanding the list of candidates learning the telegraphic code rather than limiting it. Most people have their first sensory experience with the Morse Code in visual printed form (. — .) and are only later subjected to the sound forms. Each Morse Code experience, the sight or the sound, is completely different—at different levels of experience. Unfortunately, in an effort to learn more rapidly, some people study code in the written form and that causes their difficulty in later learning the audio Morse Code.

Intelligent people can get stuck on a task, not by failing to apply themselves but by doing too well on an inappropriate level. Rather than learn by just *listening* to the code sound, they also memorize and work on the *printed* code. Then when hearing and trying to remember each sound, they mentally convert it back into what they remember seeing without first identifying the sound symbol. As examples, they would hear: dot, dot, dot, dash, dash, dash, dot, dot, dot and they would have to visualize it as ... — — — ... before recognizing the sound symbol as "SOS." This mental procedure slows up recognition and deprives one of the ability to acquire the great speed that is necessary to become a code operator. Many intelligent World War II cadet pilots failed and were forced out of pilot training because of this. It is necessary to start out immediately learning the audio code by hearing, without visualizing the letters of the telegraphic message, that is, listening for the auditory closure, the musical sound that results from musical beats of each individual letter pattern. As one becomes more proficient, each word and word cluster takes on such a significance. One hears melody rather than the individual dots and dashes. This illustrates that we are not necessarily experiencing an instant sensation with our different senses on the same levels. Such realization allows us to expand our levels and use those that are more rewarding. Helping to recall things by changing the levels and resolving learning problems at different levels are some of the rewards.

To illustrate one's potential ability to utilize fully the levels and points of view by mentally expanding the number of ways of responding to a situation, the following is offered: During the Vietnam War, at a Greenwich Village church which served as headquarters, an antiwar group built a replica of notorious tiger cages used for prisoners in South Vietnam and placed it on the church steps. To its creators, no doubt, it was a symbol of man's inhumanity to man. Not to one young vagabond, however. Several mornings in a row he could be found in his sleeping bag lying within the shelter of the tiger cage. Secure behind the bars and somewhat protected from the cold and damp, he was more secure mentally than if he were on a mere park bench. This further confirms the seventeenth century point of view of the poet, Richard Lovelace: °

> Stone walls do not a prison make,
> Nor iron bars a cage;
> Minds innocent and quiet take
> That for an hermitage

No matter what the level of abstraction, no matter what parts of the whole are considered, the basic terms structure, order and relation are inherent to any understanding.

° Richard Lovelace, "To Althea from Prison," stanza 4.

APPLICATIONS OF SKILL OF CHANGING POINT OF VIEW—YOUR ORIENTATION

In each of these three groups of proverbs, mark the one which has a different meaning from the others based on your first point of view. Then see how many different points of view you can discover.

Group 1
1. Every long journey begins with a single step.
2. Large oaks from little acorns grow.
3. Rivers from little fountains flow.
4. Little grass grows on a well-traveled road.
5. Great ends result from little starts.

Three possible types of answers:

First—number 4:   Small to big rather than big to small, on change of point of view.

Second—number 2:   Because all others deal with travel terms.

Third—number 1:   All others have "little."

Group 2
1. No man is a hero to his valet.
2. Familiarity breeds contempt.
3. If every day were sunny, who would not wish for rain?
4. Sweets grown common lose their dear delight.
5. Every breed likes best its own nest.

Group 3 {
1. Where there's smoke there's fire.
2. A single match can start a great fire.
3. A single rumor can ruin a great reputation.
4. A single slip can sink a mighty ship.
5. For want of a nail the battle was lost.
}

This test can also be used to show similarities (relations) and differences (structure). You will find when you examine each sentence with just these in mind, new points of view are evident.

PROBLEM—IN CHANGING LEVELS

Two trains are on the same track 100 miles apart heading toward one another. Each is moving at a speed of 50 miles an hour. As they start up, a bird is frightened and flies along the track at a speed of 25 miles an hour until it meets the other train which again frightens it. It reverses direction until it meets the first train, etc. What distance would the bird have covered back and forth before the two trains meet? *Answer:* 25 miles. The bird traveling at 25 m.p.h. for 1 hour, the time it takes each train to travel half the distance, each would travel a total of 50 miles. If we consider only order (passing time), the time that the bird was in flight and the time that the trains were in motion, we come to this solution.

STOP. Do you agree?

The above problem was taken from a children's arithmetic book. The problem and its solution are meaningless because on the level of the "real world" the first thing we would find is that the train traveled faster than the bird and bypassed the bird; therefore the bird could not have traveled back and forth. The problem is on a level removed from reality. We find that too many problems and studies are on such fantasy levels. Keep track of your level.

10

The Scientific Method Expanded

The greatest invention of the nineteenth century was the invention of the method of invention.
—Alfred North Whitehead

Everyone recognizes that the capacity of people, that is, what they could do, is greater than their "ability"—that is, their present level of performance. Proper training makes the difference. Creative thinking can be improved with proper training. As custodians of our creative thinking skills, we can continue to expand them. This consists of a re-awakening of the individual to heretofore unseen new possibilities by reviewing and being made aware of the use of structure, order, relation, level and point of view.

The role of conscious direction of the creative thinking process is similar to the adoption of the scientific method for solving problems. The scientific method is man's conscious codification of the unconscious, neurophysiological processes employed by all animals in solving problems. The human phenomenon known as scientific method has three steps. The first is the gathering of data; the second is the tentative formulation of new creative connections among the data, i.e., the formulation of hypotheses; and the third is the testing of the hypothesis thus created.

Why was the scientific method suitable for man's formalized creative adventures? First, it offered a nonpersonal and independently usable method for creativity. Second, the three steps in the scientific method implicitly focus on the creative thinking skills. Third, these elements fall into the following sequences: observing an occurrence, becoming aware of changes in time and place (order), seeing differences (structure), and then matching similarities (relation). Notice the scientific method sequence follows the "natural order" of evaluation as noted by Alfred Korzybski. That is, it follows the same pattern (O.S.R.) as an infant develops in discovering and understanding his environment.

Once we are aware of the natural order, we can return to Webster's definition of creation: "The act of bringing the world into existence from nothing." We as infants have literally done this in creating our personal subjective world. We as adults can change that world as often as we desire by changing structure, order, relation, level and point of view. However, the scientific method provides a method for staying in touch with the *external* world by probing and comparing with the "natural order" various aspects of the same elements of our private world.

With this awareness, the scientific investigator should be conscious when he makes deviations from the natural order of evaluation and be able to use such deviation to help him function more creatively. The scientific methodology is not inefficient in the behavioral sciences, but it has grave limitations built into it, especially in the field of psychiatry. In the various humanities, it is imitated by various quasi-scientific behavioral problem-solving methods. It has been unable to reach personal-level solutions in the industrial, commercial, educational, and factory establishments. Recognizing some of these limitations in application may give us insights into areas and directions that enlarging our scientific-method approach might make worthwhile. For example, changing patterns and problem solving may yield solutions through restating a problem as a series of subproblems (changing levels), or by starting with the goal which we wish to achieve and going backward (order). Working backward toward the start may show us methods for achieving our end.

Dr. Leo Wollman of New York was faced with a case in which one of his patients felt that, after serving several years in the armed forces, he was now too old to study and felt he could not compete with younger men in school. Dr. Wollman gave him posthypnotic suggestions to regress in time when his ability to learn was at its greatest intensity. He was then given further suggestions to study. As a result of the continual efforts of going backward in time, the patient became more confident and, subsequently, was able to pass his examinations. The order of arrangement of the subproblems also involves directions. This can involve looking at the stages and substages of the problem. A traveler looking for directions asked a mountain man how to go to Spring Mountain. After a short while he got this answer: "If I were going there I wouldn't start from here." Unfortunately most of us in trying to solve our problems are bound to the "here" and find it difficult to start from any other place. Some find the direction of the scientific method helpful, but fail to appreciate that this is but one path of the many that are open.

ATTENTIVE SOLUTIONS APPLICATIONS

The following are examples of alternative solutions to problems. Analyze each one and determine whether the solution mainly involves the creative thinking skills of using structure, relation, order, level, or point of view.

1. *Problem:* Cut down on noise from auto-horn blowing in cities.
   Alternative solution:
   Place an automobile horn inside as well as outside the auto so that when the driver blows his horn, he, as well as the other driver, is subjected to the noise blast. (Relation)

2. *Problem:* How to encourage safe driving?
   Alternative solutions:
   (a) Safe-driving campaign—supportive working with the other driver rather than defensive-driving campaign—to be on the helpful lookout for the other driver. (Relation)
   (b) Traffic officer giving credit points for good driving habits as a reward as well as present system of giving demerits for bad driving.

3. *Problem:* How can minority groups get across messages to the general public of their dissatisfaction with specific conditions?
   Alternative solution:
   Public unions with access to courts.

4. *Problem:* How can doctors and other public-service groups, without striking, tell the public about their grievances?
   Alternative solution:
   Offer their services free to the general population as a message of their grievances instead of striking and denying services.

5. *Problem:* How to control deer and other animals of the forest from eating vegetable gardens, plants and flowers around summer home?
   Alternative solution:
   Buy lion dung or other predatory animal waste from your local zoo. When it is spread around, it will discourage the deer from coming on your property.

   Using all five creative thinking skills, investigate the above problems for other solutions.

PROBLEM

Write out a problem in your field so that alternatives in all five creative thinking skills will become apparent.

Example: Suggest a number of alternate ways of treating cancerous tissue with a deadly chemical without injuring the healthy tissue.

Language and Metaphor Uses Developed

The individual's whole experience is built upon the plan of his language.

—Henri Delacroix

There can be great satisfaction in the analysis of the metaphors of great artists. Each "critic" can discover new meanings by approaching a work with a new point of view on different levels, thereby changing structure, order and relation. Shakespeare's "To be or not to be" is a fine example. We often do this unconsciously, suddenly seeing in a work of art some great design that had not been there before (and may not be there when we look again). Interpretive artists—actors, musicians and the like—can bring these intuitive comprehensions into their conscious mind and act upon them with success.

Ever since Aristotle studied the relationship between language and creative thought, widely varying theories of the relationships have been advanced.

According to popular myth, certain languages are said to be particularly appropriate for expressing specific ideas or emotions: German for logic, Italian or French (each has its partisans) for love, and, for anything, "the Greeks had the word for it." Some modern scholars, comparing a child's behavior before the appearance of language (usually about the middle of the second year) and afterward, have concluded that language is the source of thought. Piaget has challenged this notion. In his studies of child development, he takes the general position that thought can neither be reduced to language nor explained by it. However, this does not mean that Piaget believes thought and language to be independent of one another. "Once language appears, it is in constant interaction with thought. In a sense, language is to thought what mathematics is to physics, a tool and a handmaiden rather than a master. Like mathematics, language facilitates the expansion of thought and adds to its mobility. With the aid of language, thought can do much more than it would otherwise be capable of doing." °

By changing levels in examining language, we soon discover that there are different types of language within any particular language. Jeremy Bentham determined that the world consisted of entities which are either real or fictitious and that the language should be organized to deal with each of them. Ludwig Wittgenstein, in the only work published in his lifetime,† presented the then radical idea that reality is inseparable from language and can be expressed by language itself or by names, which are the "logical pictures" created by language. Later he referred to various types of language as language games. In *What is Meaning* (1903), Viola Welby formulated a general theory of meaning to create a new attitude toward experience. C.K. Ogden and I.A. Richards in *The Meaning of Meaning* expanded on her work, bringing to the study of meaning points of view drawn from other disciplines: anthropology, psychology and the physical sciences. In *Metaphor and Meaning‡*, Weller Embler considers three types of language: the language of reports, which deals with what exists in the world; the language of truths, which is used to formulate statements about reality; and the language of the arts, which is "particularly abundant of metaphorical expression." Continuing study in language and abstraction techniques will expand our creative skills even further.

° Jean Piaget, *Six Psychological Studies*, Vintage Books, 1968.
† *Tractatus Logico-Philosophicus*, 1921.
‡ Everett/Edwards, 1966.

Today, students of language have often discovered a profound link between creativity and the use of metaphor, which Aristotle realized almost 2,200 years ago when he commented: "Now strange words simply puzzle us; ordinary words convey only what we know already; it is from metaphor that we can best get hold of something fresh." ° In the nineteenth century historian Thomas Carlyle wrote, "Examine language; what, if you except some few primitive elements (of natural sound), what is it all but metaphors, recognized as such, or no longer recognized?" † He too recognized metaphor as a foundation of thought.

Unfortunately, the term "metaphor" often has conveyed to many of us a precious, esoteric, preoccupation of poets and English teachers. S.I. Hayakawa observes: "In traditional rhetoric, metaphor has long been known as a 'figure of speech'—an embellishment of literary discourse. As long as metaphors were so regarded—as merely the paper panties of one's lamb chop—they could be ignored." ‡

In this traditional sense we may recall the one thing about metaphors many of us learned in school and promptly forgot: metaphors are subtly different from similes. A simile is a comparison of two unlike things where the comparison is made obvious by the use of "like" or "as" and the relationship is explicit. Robert Burns provides a generous sample of a simile:

> *O my luve is like a red, red rose,*
> *That's newly sprung in June.*
> *O my luve is like the melodie*
> *That's sweetly play'd in tune.*

The metaphor omits "like" or "as." A word or phrase that literally denotes one kind of object or idea is used in place of

° *Metaphor and Meaning*, 1966.
† From *Sartor Resartus*, 1883.
‡ From Weller Embler, *Metaphor and Meaning*.

another to *suggest* a likeness or analogy and the relationship is implicit. John Boyle O'Reilly provides a lush nineteenth century example of a metaphor.

> *The red rose whispers of passion*
> *And the white rose breathes of love;*
> *O the red rose is a falcon*
> *And the white rose is a dove.*

This is the sort of overblown metaphor that inspired Gertrude Stein's campaign to stamp out all metaphors. "A rose is a rose is a rose," Ms. Stein insisted. And who can quarrel with her? Still there is a vast difference between her statement and those of the two other poets. Indeed, they are speaking in different languages. Ms. Stein is using what Embler would call the language of reports. To paraphrase her statement: It is structured like a rose; its order (sequence) follows the growth pattern of roses; it is related (similar) to all other roses. Therefore it *is* a rose. All of this is on a no-nonsense, literal level. There seems to be no attempt or desire to add embellishments.

The Burns and O'Reilly usage is different. In Burns the relationships are explicit—" . . . my Luve is like a . . . rose, . . . my Luve is like the melodie"—but the structures and orders are less obvious and can viewed on several different levels as parallel examples. This is one possible analysis of the point of view of Burns:

Relation I:	My Luve/rose.
Order I:	Young, vigorous, in the springtime of life.
Structure I:	Noting slight differences in temporal beauty.
Relation II:	My Luve/melodie.
Order II:	Changing in a harmonious pattern.
Structure II:	Noting the differences in transitory beauty.

O'Reilly's relationships are of course stated implicitly.

O'Reilly's point of view in metaphors might be analyzed this way:

Relation I:	Red rose/passion.
Structure I:	Secret, furtive/falcon.
Order I:	Swift bird of attack.
Relation II:	White rose/love.
Structure II:	Spontaneous, open/dove.
Order II:	To become an innocent victim.

A conclusion: passion will make a victim of love as the falcon does the dove.

Embler describes point of view when he writes: "A poet's purpose is to express his personal response to his encounter with the world. It is not the physical facts that he reports but rather the world as he believes it to be, or as he would like it to be, or hopes it may become." ° Hayakawa quotes various students as believing that "metaphor is the fundamental process by which language grows and adapts itself to the changing world . . . metaphors are the very stuff with which human beings make sense of the universe . . ." † From this it would seem that a thorough understanding of metaphors can indeed be a powerful tool for fashioning creative ideas. How to formulate them? By dividing the thoughts into structure, order and relation. In the problems that follow, you will be given the opportunity to see how metaphors, using structure, order, relation on different levels and with different points of view have been used in the past to condense the wisdom of the ages. As a punster could observe:

A man's thoughts should exceed him. For what else is a met-a-phor?

Metaphors by definition deal with similarity or relationship. According to a *New York Times* article (April 15, 1980),

---

° Weller Embler, *Metaphor and Meaning.*
† S. I. Hayakawa.

psychologists at the Institute for Cognitive Studies, Rutgers University, believe metaphors also hold clues to the nature of human creativity. "In a number of case studies of creative figures, large metaphors have been found to be linked both with the process of discovery and with the act of organizing a body of material." Although the researchers observed certain general qualities of creativity, they have not been able to tell *why* they are important. The Art of Creative Thinking™ offers a ready answer: metaphors deal not only with relation, but with order ("the process of discovery") and structure ("the act of organizing a body of material"). The psychologists, limited by the literal meaning of "metaphor," saw it in only one creative dimension: relation. A "good" metaphor should encompass all three: structure, order *and* relation.

To get a clearer understanding of the process, consider clichés. They are nothing more than metaphors that have outlived their usefulness. Take "mad as a wet hen," for example. If you have ever seen a wet hen, you will recognize that the metaphor is perfectly apt. A hen caught in the rain is the personification of helpless fury. Fifty years ago most people would recognize the image. Today, hens are caged indoors under carefully controlled conditions and work on an assembly line that produces eggs. When their production declines they end up in the supermarket, plucked and headless (hence, no expression). They aren't even given the dignity of their correct name: old hen. Instead they are called "fowl."

Why is this metaphor a cliché? Consider change—order.

1. The *structure* has changed. Formerly the comparison was between an angry person and a hen that *looked* angry. Now when they meet, the hen is "as naked as a jaybird" (no wet feathers) and the person is usually, as before, clothed.

2. The *order* has changed. Formerly the hen's appearance

changed when it got wet. Now it doesn't get wet but the person still looks angry.

3. The *relation* has changed. Formerly the hen was free to roam as much as it pleased, just like a person. Now it is under strict supervision.

Some metaphors are timeless; most become clichés. How would you classify the following and why?

"Nothing is seen clearly and certainly by a man in a hurry; haste is improvident and blind."—Livy

"For a man indeed ought not to cover his head forasmuch as he is the image and glory of God; but the woman is the glory of the man."—I Corinthians #11:7

"What the French call Christian milk—milk which has been baptized."—Mark Twain

" 'Tis a base, ignoble mind
That mounts no higher than a bird can soar."—Shakespeare

"To tell tales out of school: that is her great lust."—John Heywood

"It is perfectly monstrous the way people go about nowadays saying things against one, behind one's back, that are absolutely and entirely true."—Oscar Wilde

"The heavens themselves, the planets, and this centre
Observe degrees, proportion, season, form, office and custom,
in all line of order."—Shakespeare

"The mouth of a cannon is safer than the mouth of a slanderer." —Arab proverb

"The air of England has long been too pure for a slave, and every man is free who breathes it."—Lord Mansfield: *Judgement in the Case of James Somersett, a Negro, 1772*

"England is a prison for men, a paradise for women, a purgatory for servants, a hell for horses."—Thomas Fuller, 1642

"Malice is cunning."—Cicero

"Malice is blind."—Livy

"A bad marriage is like an electrical thrilling machine: it makes you dance, but you can't let go,"—Ambrose Bierce, 1911

"There comes Poe with his raven like Barnaby Rudge,
Three-fifths of him genius, and two-fifths sheer fudge."—J. R. Lowell

EXERCISES

Metaphors and Meaning Applications

Using the creative thinking skills:

a) Examine the parts of each proverb and look for similarities, differences and changes.

b) Now compare the one part of the set to the other, considering Structure (S), Order (O) and Relation (R):

1. "Every cloud has a silver lining."
   "It never rains but it pours."

   Order—clouds come before rain, therefore do something before it rains.

2. "Absence makes the heart grow fonder."
   "Out of sight, out of mind."

   Relation (compare structure)—the heart behaves differently from the mind.

3. "Make hay while the sun shines."
   "Rome wasn't built in a day."

   Relation—different periods of time (order) require different considerations.

4. "Look before you leap."
   "He who hesitates is lost."

   Order—can there be a time period appropriate to both?

You may have observed that the preceding proverbs are also metaphors. With this insight, continue to examine the structure, order and relation of the following proverb-metaphors and you will begin to see how wise men in the past have distilled the "truths" of their world. Then use your own unique point of view to create metaphors of your own.

5. "Keep your nose to the grindstone."
   "All work and no play makes Jack a dull boy."

6. "Two heads are better than one."
   "Too many cooks spoil the broth."

7. "A penny saved is a penny earned."
   "Penny wise and pound foolish."

8. "Don't put all your eggs in one basket."
   "Jack of all trades, master of none."

9. "Don't burn the candle at both ends."
   "Experience is the best teacher."

10. "Good fences make good neighbors."
    "The grass is always greener on the other side of the fence."

11. "Nothing ventured, nothing gained."
    "Better safe than sorry."

12. "Many hands make light work."
    "If you want something done well, do it yourself."

13. "Where there's smoke, there's fire."
    "All that glitters is not gold."

14. "Big oaks from little acorns grow."
    "One swallow doesn't make a summer."

15. "The early bird gets the worm."
    "Better late than never."

16. "A friend in need is a friend indeed."
    "Charity begins at home."

17. "Cast your bread upon the waters."
"Waste not, want not."

18. "Stolen water tastes sweetest."
"Drink from your own cistern."

19. "Beggars can't be choosers."
"The meek shall inherit the earth."

By changing the levels above, can you see new sets of structure, order and relation?

Suggested answers ⟶
1. a
2. c
3. a
4. a or b
5. b

PICTURE ANALOG

12

Classification Methods Re-examined and Expanded

When we start to learn, we classify everything, using differences and/or similarities. This is the result of our experience or inference from others' experience. After a while, we tend to think of classification as something existing in nature based upon something inherent in structures. Much academic work has been done on so-called "natural" classification systems. It would appear that there are no natural systems inherent in nature—only results of man-made systems. We use classifications based upon what we have projected into structures, not something that is inherent in them. The basis for the belief in "true" relationships arises from Aristotle, who essentially sought relationship according to his concepts of natural order. While there appears to be natural order in classifications, such as the spectrum of colors or geometrical figures, upon deeper consideration even these formulations can be seen as systems which we have created and equipped with "natural" order. We discount in "nature" the existence of a reverse rainbow as not natural.

A school librarian developed a method to help children recognize some problems in classification. They were asked to bring in a banana or other fresh fruit, the fresher the better. A color classification system was organized. They were asked to put the fruit under its "proper" color classification. Each week the class was invited to inspect the stored fruit. After several weeks the children realized a factor that they had not considered. What systems of classification have allowances for change (order) built into them? Our classifications usually do not allow for life's continual changing.

Restated: in man-made conceptual systems such as physical sizes, social orders or mathematics, we impose a series of classifications, and then respond to a hierarchy as though it had some natural order. As an illustration, try to think of a "natural" way to classify smells. We are deluded to think we achieve this when we discover in these "natural" classification systems some similarity to life, an invariance under transformaton, something isomorphic about the mental system in relation to our precepts of the outside objective world. The success of a classification system is measured by how well it predicts occurrences and teaches us aspects of the outside world that we had not considered or discovered. As suggested by Kurt Gödel, the mathematician, in mathematics no system can be 100 per cent true. We unknowingly are forced to accept many areas of inaccuracies in our classifications.

Every human being is born into a culture with extensive classification systems. These we adopt with little if any re-examination. Our worlds are then based upon such classifications. As a result, we see largely those characteristics that the person who originated the classification system looked for and integrated. Understanding structure, order and relation can be most helpful in analyzing various types of relationship and classification that we may be exposed to. We can then re-examine them based upon our need at the particular time, and can change them. We are not frozen into past intuition of a "natural" system.

Consider West Publishing Company, a law book publisher, which, beginning in 1880, digested and classified the law throughout the United States to assist lawyers in doing legal research. However, over the years, the classification became rigid. The law was classified under specific subject headings; these became the structures. This inadvertently put blinders on law students, lawyers doing research, and legislators seeking to change the law. It forced them to think in accordance with these limited numbers of categories. They were trapped by the pigeonholes of labels. Today, West Publishing has 427 topics and 83,000 key numbers. As some completely new concepts in the law developed, new subject headings were added, such as Workmen's Compensation and Administrative Law, but in essence the main body of law remained static. It also gave rise to some archaic usage, because the system still retains such subject headings as Bastardy—and people do not usually think of law in such terms.

Systems are to be utilized whenever possible but we should always realize their limitations. In most instances the original classifiers failed to take advantage of *all five* of our creative skills. We who have inherited these classifications should not feel constrained from changing them.

The next chapter will help us go beyond such limitations.

APPLICATION OF CLASSIFICATIONS

Clustering Methods and Methods of Classification

(Applications to discover alternative classifications)

Organize the following dot cluster first into groups of 2, then into groups of 3, and finally into groups of 4:

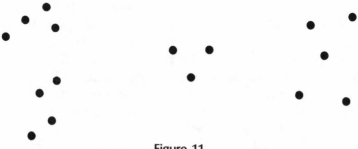

Figure 11

After you have connected the dots, examine the basis of the reasons for making your selections. Can you see other ways of classifying them? By changing point of view, can new relations be seen? Has a failure to use these limited your past classification?

Classifying Objects

Classify in any way you consider appropriate the following items:

1. Finishing nail
2. Box nail
3. Thumbtack
4. Upholstery tack
5. Wood screw
6. Metal screw
7. Bolt

Consider why you used the method that you chose to classify the objects. Can you classify them in any other way? What are the relational factors used to classify them? Can you now classify them using other forms of relationship? Can you change levels and see other relationships? Each new way of classifying expands the uses of the systems.

Analyzing your preferences for systems of classification will allow you to discover habitual patterns that may be changed. Did you analyze them in accordance with the words or the objects that they represented? Did you find similarities between the words, alphabetizing them, for example? Did you then cluster those objects, finding various linkages between the words? Did you have difficulty with one object that was in a separate category and did not fit into the classification? Could there not be another method of classifying the objects so that they would be included in some relationship with the order?

Awareness and thereafter overcoming the limits of your categories and methods of classification add to the art of creative thinking.

Some of the more obvious limits are:

1. Your purpose in classifying.
2. The hidden factors which determine your classification.
3. Choosing inappropriate S.O.R. for the present classification.
4. Choosing only one point of view and/or level.
5. Choosing old familiar categories and their subdivisions.

EXERCISES

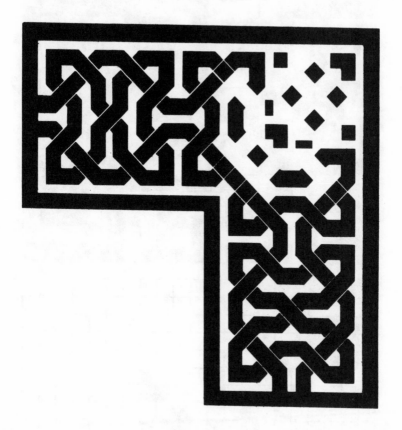

Figure 12

This design is incomplete. See if you can complete it in a way that is consistent with the artist's intent. Compare your solution with the one given in Figure 14, page 135.

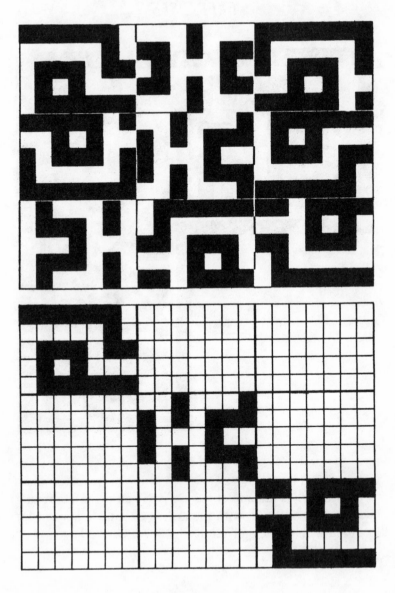

Figure 13

The Fret is made up of nine rectangular blocks as shown in the upper half of the illustration. However, only three of the blocks are placed in the correct position as shown in the lower half. Try to make a perfect Fret out of the three correctly placed blocks and the six incorrectly placed without turning any of the blocks around. Compare your solution with Figure 15, page 136.

Figure 14

This is the solution that matches the classification of the artist in completing Figure 12.

Figure 15

Since most of the squares along the top and bottom of the correctly positioned blocks are black, it is logical to classify two blocks with a preponderance of black squares on the top and two with the same on the bottom. Trial and error with the other two blocks will complete the design.

GEOMETRIC CLASSIFICATION—CAN YOU DISCOVER ALTERNATIVE NAMES FOR THE DIFFERENT CATEGORIES?

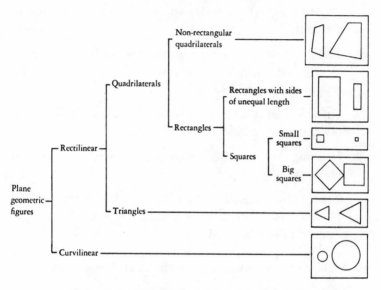

Copyright © 1980 by Gerard I. Nierenberg

After exhausting your alternatives, read on.

Turn page ninety degrees clockwise. Do the illustrations suggest new categories? For example: Big Mama—Little Mama?
Going my way?
Balancing act?
Camera?
TV set?
Broken TV set?

Our senses are usually limited to the classifications listed below. Consider ways to expand them.

1. *Taste:* The taste buds can only distinguish between sweet, sour, salt or bitter—or a combination of any of the four.

2. *Smell:* There are only a few basic odors (perhaps seven in all) that your nose can distinguish, but many combinations are possible.

3. *Sight:* Vision is limited to certain light wavelengths and intensity of the light source.

4. *Hearing:* We can hear sounds only within a limited range of wavelengths.

5. *Touch:* Our sense of touch is basic to understanding the physical world (children, especially, rely on it), but it is limited to the "near at hand."

Hint: How do electronic and mechanical means expand our senses?

PICTURE CLASSIFICATION

See answers on next page.

Suggested answers
1. c   Support
2. c   Measuring devices
3. b   Article handled when used
4. a   Soft thing (also smoke soft)
5. b   Organisms
6. a   Objects capable of holding or carrying fluids
7. b   Unfinished thing
8. c   Mythological people
9. a   Tools which are turned and twisted
10. c   Objects consumed

IV

Your Abilities Increased With Exercises in Life's Problems

To recognize a problem which can be solved and is worth solving is . . . a discovery in its own right.

Michael Polanyi, *Personal Knowledge*

13

Research More
Creatively

As is your sort of mind,
So is your sort of search; you'll find
What you desire.
—Robert Browning, "Easter Day"

In a cartoon, two lawyers are standing in a great legal library surrounded by books. One says, "Well, one thing you can be sure of. It's here someplace." At one time or another we have all been confronted with this feeling of near impotence, a variation on the Ancient Mariner's observation:

Water, water, every where,
Nor any drop to drink.

Librarians and experienced researchers are generally quite knowledgeable about where certain kinds of facts may be found. This is because they have mastered many purely arbitrary classification systems various scholars have used to organize and file compilations of information. Generally, these filing systems deal with only one concept: structure or order or relation, and fail to distinguish different levels of knowing and points of view. For example, English language dictionaries are arranged according to structure—words—which are listed in alphabetical order and differentiated as being verbs, nouns, adjectives or other grammatical classifications. Unabridged dictionaries will also give some of the other mental concepts, each word's order, relation and a few levels of use, but most short dictionaries do not. Thus you would not go to a short dictionary to find out *how* to use a word but only to discover *what* it means—or, put another way, differences between it and the other words listed.

Some dictionaries do attempt to apply the five creative mental skills by having seven basic kinds of definitions:

1. *Synonym:* deals with structures (same level).

2. *Antonym:* deals with relation-opposite (same level).

3. *Exemplification:* pointing at a particular structure—actually or with words.

4. *Comparison:* structure (same level).

5. *Classification:* gives the class and the differentiations from the others in the class.

6. *Structure analysis:* how it fits into the structure—e.g., finger on hand.

7. *Operation analysis:* structure change in time and space (order); stage, phase, junction, function, purpose.

Other examples of alternative ways of defining words are:

Definition considers *structure* if in terms of genus and species.

Definition considers *relation* if in terms of whole and parts.

Definition considers *order* if in terms of stages or concept of function and purpose.

Some of the weaknesses of a classification system are illustrated by *The Dictionary of American Biography* and its British counterpart, *The Dictionary of National Biography.* They mainly deal with similarities or relationships. All entries are born or naturalized American or British citizens. (The content of the individual biographies concern orders, structures and levels. Also, no one ever has the pleasure of looking himself up in DAB or DNB. You must be dead to make it.) This biographical information can be added to if you go to other sources.

For example, you might be interested in, say, a nineteenth century American poet who wrote *Wynken, Blynken and Nod.* The *New Century Cyclopedia of Names,* for example, would be necessary to give you this information because, like a language dictionary, it is classified according to terms of structure: the name of the poem and the poet are listed in alphabetical order and as separate entries. Another possible source but less accessible than NCCN might be an anthology of American verse which would classify according to the terms of relation (all are poems) and level (all are "good" poems), but you would have to know another relation, that the poet was an American. (Answer: Eugene Field)

A dictionary of synonyms and a crossword puzzle dictionary are examples of classification by relations and orders. They suggest how you may change words (relation) by merely changing degrees (order) of meaning. In a synonyms dictionary, listed under the word "intimidate," we find "browbeat, bulldoze, bully, cow, daunt, dismay, overawe and terrorize."

What has research to do with creative thinking? First, effective research involves an all-out hunt for structures, orders, relations, levels and points of view. So does the search for creative solutions. Second, as Sir Isaac Newton observed some three hundred years ago (in 1676), one can see farther by standing on the shoulder of giants. This is a gracious and modest way of acknowledging that we could scarcely find time to be even creative if we were unable to utilize and build upon the past, to take advantage of cumulative points of view.

Newton's epigram can provide an instructive example of the uses and abuses of research. Let us suppose you want to "stand on the shoulder of giants" by quoting Newton's exact words. *Bartlett's Familiar Quotations,* Fourteenth Edition, will probably provide them. How do you find the quotations? You can look under Newton (structure), in the Index of Authors, which will direct you to page 379. There the first entry under Newton is the quotation, "If I have seen farther (than you and Descartes) it is by standing upon the shoulders of Giants." (Letter to Robert Hooke, February 5, 1675/6.) Do not let the date bother you. It is the way the Old Style or Julian Calendar expressed a year that began on March 1. In the New Style or Gregorian Calendar, the year would be 1676, but Great Britain did not adopt the new calendar until 1752. What is worrisome is the footnote which reads "See Lucan, p. 134a and Robert Burton, p. 310a." Since these pages precede Newton's and the authors are arranged chronologically, it would seem possible, considering order, that Newton was "standing on the shoulders of giants" (Lucan and Burton) when coining his epigram.

We might confirm this by looking up the two authors, but there are alternate ways. Suppose you did not know that Newton had made the statement. Then you would use the index of key words. Under "Giant" you would find "dwarf on shoulder of g." and under "Giants," "pygmies on shoulders of g." and "standing upon shoulders of g." Under "Shoulders" are "dwarf on s. of giant, pygmies on s. of giants, standing on s. of giants." These in turn direct you to Lucan, Burton and Newton. Lucan, a Roman writer who was forced to commit suicide because Nero didn't like him, said, according to Bartlett's translation, "Pygmies placed on the shoulders of giants see more than the giants themselves." Also according to Bartlett, the quotation is from *The Civil War, Book II, 10 (Didacus Stella).* Robert Burton, whose most famous work is *Anatomy of Melancholy,* is quoted thus: "I say with Didacus Stella, a dwarf standing on the shoulders of a giant may see farther than a giant himself."

Who, you might ask, is Didacus Stella? Fortunately that question and many others are answered in a delightful book,

On the Shoulders of Giants by Robert K. Merton. As the jacket describes it, "Merton gives the reader a diverting (and often, digressing) guided tour through a well-stocked mind. His literary detective work carries him through science, philosophy, literature, musicology, religion, economics, sociology and psychology. Among other things he discovers that Lucan never said what Bartlett's says he did. This is one of the common pitfalls of research: the printed word is not necessarily accurate or the truth. He also discovers no less than forty-seven versions of the epigram ranging from Bernard of Chartres in 1126 to Sigmund Freud in the twentieth century. The last, to quote Merton, "came to pass when Stekel, that unwanted disciple of Freud and regarded by him as a conscienceless pretender to science, tried to make self-interested use of the aphorism. Stekel had become thoroughly persuaded that his ideas surpassed those of the master. He liked to express this by saying, with arrogant modesty, that a dwarf on the shoulders of a giant can of course see farther than the giant himself. Comes then the giant's crusher when he hears of this claim: 'That may be true, but a louse on the head of a philosopher does not.' "

What in essence are Merton's methods for untangling this web of confusion? Quite simply, a relentless and tireless search pattern (point of view) that discovers new and more valid uses of structures, orders, relations and levels.

A lawyer can approach the research library file systems using the same techniques of searching for points of view, levels, structures, orders and relations. Take this problem: An uncle writes his seventeen-year-old nephew that if he stops smoking until he is twenty-one, the uncle will give him $10,000. The nephew stops smoking, but when he reaches twenty-one, the uncle refuses to give him the money. He says it was for the nephew's own good. Does the nephew have a valid claim against the uncle?

Research may be done under the terms of structure (different words): uncle, nephew, smoking. Under relation (similarities), it could be: gift and relatives. Under order (changes), one could try: reaching majority (18-21) or the change that the nephew made as a result of the uncle's request. The action of the nephew, who could have smoked or stopped smoking, is referred to in the law as "consideration." The use of just three of the creative skills gives you many alternative insights into the research for a solution. The judge's decision, for the record, is that when the nephew voluntarily gave up the right to smoke, even though it may have been for his own benefit, was consideration. A written contract had been made that was enforceable.

The British humorist Jerome K. Jerome, in *Three Men in a Boat—Not to Mention a Dog* (1889) gives a classic example of the layman searching for a medical diagnosis. In this case, the narrator comes to the firm conclusion that he suffers from Housemaid's Knee. Fortunately, most medical research is done on a sounder basis. However, when an average practitioner may wish to research quickly to confirm his diagnosis and proposed treatment, he can find such information in the *Merck Manual* (or, if the patient is an animal, the *Merck Veterinary Manual*). These volumes fortunately are restricted in sale to professionals, otherwise a researcher like Jerome K. Jerome using an older edition of the *Merck Manual* might have found he suffered from Bargeman's Bottom and not Housemaid's Knee at all. For an M.D. or a D.V.M., however, the manual uses terms of relation to classify various disorders: allergy, lymphatic and cardiovascular systems, digestive system, infectious diseases, metabolic disturbances, and so on. Structure is indicated under each individual entry, which covers etiology, clinical findings, diagnosis, prophylaxis and treatment. These entries also are order when they deal with stages of the condition. Since many diseases, particularly in their early stages, display similar symptoms (syphilis is notorious for this), a doctor would need to observe the "order" of the disease—the changes that take place as it progresses—to confirm his diagnosis.

Unfortunately, doctors and lawyers, as well as the many other researchers today, do not fully use their creative thinking skills and thorough research for the fruitful alternatives in the file systems that are available.

QUESTIONS FOR RESEARCH

The following questions can be answered by creative use of your library's resources. No "correct" answers can be given because the "truth" can be arrived at from many different paths. Your answer (point of view) is "correct" if you have used your awareness of the terms of structure, order, relation and level to reach it. A possible method of approach, however, is given for each question.

1. Hong Kong was leased to the British government by China. Suppose you wanted to see the provisions of the "lease" to determine its duration, area covered, etc. Where could you find a copy?

   Possible answer: Concentrate on the filing under structures of Hong Kong and Great Britain. This will lead you to the international level for research. The relation would be lessor and lessee. Therefore, the "lease" will be in the form of an agreement signed by China and Great Britain. Copies will be found in the archives of both countries. Considering other relations (available sources of information), the British Information Service in New York City also has the text of the treaty complete with map.

2. Your favorite author has written a short story with a sentence that does not make sense. You suspect it is a printer's error. However, when you write the publisher, he tells you this is the way it has appeared in every edition and is the way the author wrote it. The author is no longer living. How can you verify the sentence?

   Possible answer: Research concentrating first under the

filings on order (time, change) will enable you to retrace the progress of the book from author's manuscript to first edition. Assuming the publisher is correct in saying every edition is the same (although it might be worth a check), the story might have been printed in a magazine before it appeared in book form. Your librarian can tell you how to find out. If not, you might try to locate the original manuscript. Chances are good that some library—probably a university library—will have most if not all of the author's manuscripts. On another level your library will have this information.

3. When Pope Gregory reformed the calendar in 1582 he dropped ten days from the first year and decreed certain changes in the observance of leap year. As we have said, Britain (and her colonies including the American ones) did not adopt the new calendar until 170 years later. How many days were dropped for the year 1752 in Great Britain and her possessions?

Possible answer: You can find the structure of the calendar by looking it up in a good encyclopedia. However, it may not even mention the answer to your question. An easier way is relating order to find the Old Style date of George Washington's birthday and comparing it with the New Style date of February 22. Where? Probably in *The Dictionary of American Biography*. If not, and remembering relationship, look in *The Dictionary of National Biography* (remember the British counterpart). After all, Washington *was* a British subject during two thirds of his life span.

14

Developing Insights into Levels of Moral Education

Moral education is impossible without the habitual vision of greatness.

—Alfred North Whitehead

Jean Piaget's ideas about cognitive and moral judgment development in children have had wide influence far beyond the boundaries of formal education. One reason is that these ideas provide a classification of human development that can be applied to many diverse areas. They have an additional merit: although the various stages are necessarily arranged in a hierarchical order, no value judgment is necessarily intended. Each stage must be gone through chronologically and each is not only valuable but necessary for growth. The thing that differentiates a "higher" from a "lower" stage (level) is that its principles (points of view) have applicability over a broader range of human experience.

The relatively new field of moral education, as opposed to indoctrination, provides interesting insights into how Piaget's theories of growth and development can be applied by others to areas outside the customary limits of formal education. Lawrence Kohlberg, a developmental psychologist, has derived these six stages of moral reasoning from Piaget. Note the changing levels and points of view:

1. The individual simply calculates what will please a par-

ental or other authority figure in order to avoid punishment.

2. The individual develops a sense of other people and discovers the benefits of reciprocity.

3. Awareness of other people takes the form of loyalty to a small group, such as a gang or team.

4. The individual recognizes that his own rights and those of others must be balanced by his society's need for law and order.

5. A person is willing to challenge the law occasionally in the interest of "higher" subjective principles.

6. Fidelity to universal principles and respect for human rights are paramount considerations.

As with any educational theory or method, there are dissenters and critics of Kohlberg's ideas but relatively few deny that these six steps correspond to the changes that take place in child development. It also seems probable that adults operate on different levels to meet varying needs and that a vastly greater number of adults will confine themselves to the lower levels, probably Steps 1 through 4, than will ever attempt to reach Steps 5 and 6.

What seems most obviously to change as one goes from step 1 to step 6 is relation, the situations we can empathize with, the broadening of our point of view. As we move up the levels, our concern and involvement with others is enlarged. The first ("They behaved like the medieval peasants praying to St. Florian: 'God and Father, if Thy thunder strikes, let it be my neighbor's house, not mine.' ") is the relationship of a subordinate to a superior; the second, two equals agreeing, "You scratch my back and I'll scratch yours." The third is a relation between an individual and a small group; the fourth, between an individual and a large group or society. In the fifth, the individual relates more to ideas than to other people. In the sixth, he achieves a broad relation with ideas *and* humanity.

As the world of relations of an individual increases, so less obviously do the changes (order) and differences (structure) become more complicated. This emerges most clearly in step 4 where "law and order" are the equivalent of structure and order. In step 1, the frozen nonchanging order is authoritarian and the structure, a concentration of power.

Add to this a superior-subordinate relation and you will see how each element (S.O.R.) is dependent on the others. We can travel in a circle in either direction to define Step 1 (see Figure 16).

In Step 2, order starts to change. Any changes (order) must be reciprocal, the structure, one to one, and the relation between equals. Again order, structure and relationship are parts of an indivisible whole.

Figure 16

Step 3: Structure is a group, order forms a group, and relation deals with similar group loyalty. All have been enlarged to include a group.

Thus far, terms of structure, order and relation have seemed relatively simple to apply, so much so that they are practically clichés. The reason is that we learn these patterns very early in life and unconsciously we expect them to "work" each time we employ them. Quite frequently they do not work. Take, for example, the New York police sergeant with an Irish brogue who tried to talk an Irish robber into surrendering. "I used my famous 'Father Gilroy' routine," he explained later. "You know, 'I'd like to speak to you, lad.' " The robber responded with a curse and fired a round of bullets, grazing the sergeant's neck, nose and ear. "Apparently he's a Protestant Irishman and he doesn't like priests," he concluded philosophically, discarding his Step 3 approach.

Step 4 has become an emotionally charged issue, a battleground for liberals and conservatives. Looked at more dispassionately it can be seen as a logical step in a hierarchy based on ever-broadening use of relations and point of view, in this case, the relation of an individual with his own social group. No society could exist in the absence of law and order and without the willingness of a majority of its members to make certain sacrifices for what it considers a social good. The circularity of this closed system might be viewed in this way: in terms of structure, fixed social relation; order, nonchanging social structure; relation, continuing social order. This stage is the epitome of status quo and conservatism with a small "c." If you attempt even the smallest change in structure, order, or relation, then society itself must change—a concept that the majority is not likely to accept with equanimity. Tradition is a byword. The majority much prefers heroes like Karl F. Meyer, the internationally famous veterinarian and public health scientist, who can do their job, no matter what, and do it well. As reported by Paul de Kruif, Meyer once bet his colleagues that unassisted and wearing a tuxedo he could do a complete autopsy of an elephant and not get a drop of blood on his shirtfront. He won. Only if things are working well for practitioners of Step 4, can they say with the poet: "God's in His heaven—all's right with the world."

One of the great examples of Step 5 in world literature is the Greek tragedy *Antigone* by Sophocles. Here the Princess Antigone defies the orders of her uncle the king and buries the body of her brother as religion demanded. For her, divine law must take precedence over man-made decrees. The outcome is as miserable as can be. Antigone is buried alive, and her lover, the king's only son, kills himself. Obviously, Step 5 involves change through challenge that can create highly unstable situations and much tragedy. This is especially true when no attempt is made for accommodating conflicting points of view through the methods available to that society.

Congressmen, in often futile attempts to screw up their courage, like to quote from an election speech Edmund Burke made to his constituents in Bristol: "Your representative owes you, not his industry only, but his judgment; and he betrays instead of serving you if he sacrifices it to your opinion." This is a bid for the voters to let him go from Step 4 to Step 5. It is usually forgotten that Burke lost the bid and the election. However, in Burke's case, there was a happy ending. Abandoning for a moment his new approach to representative government, Burke sought a new constituency and returned to Parliament.

It is almost impossible to attach labels to the terms of structure, order and relation contained in Step 5, which is characterized by volatility and is often accompanied by cries of outrage from believers in the status quo (at Step 4). It attempts to change levels and substitute an individual's point of view for the accepted social viewpoint. Sometimes it succeeds and when it does, a new structure, order and relation evolves. Often this is a challenge of the moment, suddenly arrived at but thereafter it must be doggedly pursued.

This is not true of Step 6. As with Step 4, an equilibrium is established at a new high level and broad point of view. New uses of the terms structure, order and relation change the world and one's way of looking at it (point of view). Let's return to Edmund Burke for an example of Step 6—a universal statement on mankind and principles. In 1774 he delivered his first "Speech on Conciliation with America." Two hundred years later it still is valid.

> Reflect how you govern a people who think they ought to be free, and think they are not. Your scheme yields no revenue; it yields nothing but discontent, disorder, disobedience; and such is the state of America that after wading up to your eyes in blood, you could only end just where you began; that is, to tax where no revenue is to be found, to—my voice fails me; my inclination indeed carries me no farther—all is confusion beyond it.

Lest this may seem like a lucky guess of what might happen in the future, consider Burke's prophecy about America made a month before the first shots of the Revolution were fired and more than three months before the Declaration of Independence:

> Young man, there is America—which at this day serves for little more than to amuse you with stories of savage men and uncouth manners; yet shall, before you taste of death, show itself equal to the whole of that commerce [Britain's] which now attracts the envy of the world.

Here is a mind that accepts the new and with great wisdom applies universal principles to see the world, not only as it is but as it was destined to be.

Could one use these concepts of moral reasoning, and see how they might apply to the story told by Professor Alain C. Enthoven of Stanford University? It is about a man who left the presidency of a medical products company to become a professor of management. One day he decided it would be fun to see some of his old associates from business days, so he organized a lunch at a fine restaurant. At the end of the meal, from habit, he reached for the check, but his successor as company president took it and said, "Let me have it. For us it's a deductible expense and the government will pay half of it through reduced corporate profits tax." But the local hospital administrator took it out of his hand, saying, "No, let me take it; this will be an allowable conference expense, and we can put the whole thing in our overhead and get it back from Blue Cross and Medicare." But his neighbor took the check from him and said, "Let me have it. After all, I'm a cost-plus contractor to the government and not only will we get the cost reimbursed, but we'll get a fee on top of it." But the fifth man at the table got the check: "Look, friends, I'm from a regulated industry, and we're about to go in for a rate increase. If I can put this lunch in our cost base, it will help justify a higher rate not only this year, but projected on out into the future!"

Although Kohlberg's moral reasoning is organized into a hierarchy of values, this story reverses the hierarchical "values" rather like Dante imagines the structure of hell: an inverted cone with Satan in the place of honor at the bottom. Unfortunately, this reversal of values is all too often clearly seen by the small taxpayer as he tries to relate the results of big business tax procedures to the large tax bite out of his income.

15

Increase Your Creative Negotiating Alternatives with Episodes and Exercises

A recent news item announced that Burt Shulman of Hyde Park, New York, had invented a boost for runners. A one-horsepower, two-cycle engine mounted on a backpack provides a pushing action through pads attached to the thighs. When last seen Mr. Shulman was doing 20 m.p.h. His previous inventions included ultrasonic tweezers for permanent removal of ingrown hairs; a device that provides fresh air for motorists caught in traffic jams; a gadget that blows smoke away from people using soldering guns; an alarm-clock radio that senses when it is going to rain or snow and rings earlier than usual; a device that continuously moves feet up and down to improve the circulation of desk-bound executives.

By contrast, look at the rigid thinking involved where a Wells Fargo truck was robbed of three million dollars after three of the four guards were waylaid in a Staten Island delicatessen and forced to give up their keys. Exactly twenty-four hours later a Wells Fargo truck was parked in front of the same deli and three guards were having coffee.

Probably the greatest deterrent to creative thinking is in not recognizing that, like the guards, we have a problem that needs a solution. At the other extreme are the innately creative who recognize problems and enjoy the challenge and possible rewards of solving them. Most of us fall between the two extremes. We recognize the problem but are at a loss to make a creative leap that will bring a solution.

Once you have a basic idea of the use of order, structure and relation, any number of techniques can help you become a self-starter in creatively solving problems. Let us start with the strategies you already employ to move others (and yourself) toward change. Below I will list some of the common strategies, taken from my books on negotiating, define them and then show how by changing your thinking of order, structure and relation you may find a new solution. Since we are dealing with a three-dimensional conceptual phenomenon, "knowing" what to do, it is not important to follow a strict sequence of analysis. You may find the strategy works best for you when you first consider structure or order or relation. It does not matter any more than whether you first look at depth, height or width. You only "see" dimension when all three are merged. Examples emphasizing each segment will be provided for individual strategies.

BLAND WITHDRAWAL

When you are not satisfied with your progress in solving a problem, you leave the arena perhaps to start a new game on more favorable terrain.

Order. By changing terrain, you gain a new point of view. Now look for alternatives: How can you rearrange time and/ or space to achieve a more favorable circumstance?

Structure. You examine each element—rules, people, place or circumstance—of the situation to discover which ones displeased you, then ask yourself what things would be different if you changed the terrain.

Relation. From a new point of view, you will see similarities in certain aspects of your old problem and your new situation. Ask yourself if these are helpful or harmful. Perhaps you do not like to play marbles. Maybe you should switch to chess.

Example. To return to those Wells Fargo guards: Tad Adamowski in a letter to *The New York Times* offered two solutions:

> Surprisingly, neither Wells Fargo nor government insurance has thought of equipping the armored cars with a kitchen and a cook to keep the guards from starvation, a paltry outlay compared with losses in millions.

In this solution, when order is considered, the viewpoint has shifted from that of the guards with their desperate need for coffee and Danish at a certain time each day to that of the public, who must eventually foot the bill for three million dollars. Now an alternative can be found: change the space, much as you might rearrange the furniture. Relation: the similarity between a train and an armored truck is noted, as is the need of passengers of both for refreshments. The structure: what is the difference between an armored car and a train? One has a diner, of course.

> Alternatively (Mr. Adamowski continues), perhaps there could be recruited men of exceptional stamina able to make the trip (less than an hour) from Staten Island to lower Manhattan without stopping for refreshment. They might be compensated for this hardship at, say, a thousand dollars an hour, and it would still be a bargain.

In this solution, the similarity (relation) between an exorbitant wage scale and an equally excessive loss of three million dollars is noted. After all, the loss would pay for 3,000 hours of "hard" labor. Change in time (order) is taken into account: It is better to get 3,000 hours of labor rather than nothing. The difference (structure) between stopping and going offers a pleasing creative solution.

APPARENT WITHDRAWAL

You want others to feel that your present position is a strong one. However, they do not agree with your point of view. To change their attitude you appear to withdraw ("They'll be sorry when I'm gone").

Order. You are in control of time. Temporarily you thus appear to remove yourself from the scene. However, while you make a change in space (order), you are still very much aware of the problem and are in a position to find alternative solutions. You can and will return any time it is appropriate.

Structure. By changing positions you are now looking at the problem from the outside. This will make you more aware of the differences of the problem—when creative solutions become possible.

Relation. You discover the similarity (relation) between the strength you seemed to relinquish and the strength your new outside position gives you. The strengths can be the same— only your ability to use them, the leverage of position, has changed.

Example. Andrew Jackson was a self-made man who fought his way to wealth and the Presidency, yet retained the love and respect of the common man. He reciprocated those feelings for virtually all—except the Indians. Like most frontiersmen who had fought them, he despised them. He supported the state of Georgia in its efforts to deprive the Cherokee Indians of their land. When the Georgia legislature sought to expand state jurisdiction to the Cherokee Nation, the Indians appealed to the Supreme Court, presided over by Jackson's formidable opponent, John Marshall. In 1832 the court ruled against Georgia and stated that the federal government has exclusive jurisdiction over Indian affairs. Jackson is then supposed to have said, "John Marshall has made his decision. Now let him enforce it." Whether those were his words or not, by the end of Jackson's second administration the U.S. Army had forcibly removed all Indians east of the Mississippi

River to their "permanent homeland" in Indian Territory (now Oklahoma).

Note that this creative solution (however reprehensible) deals with the structure—the difference between the powers of the Presidency and the Supreme Court. Both are great but still limited. The President cannot enforce his will without the support of Congress and/or the Executive Branch—and Jackson was in control of both. Jackson had apparently withdrawn when he refused to use the powers of the Presidency (he usually used them to the hilt), yet he did not relinquish them to anyone else. He also saw the similarities (relation) between using his powers, to be the first "strong" President in the nation's history, and withholding them. Both were acts of strength.

REVERSAL

You buck the popular trend. You do the exact opposite of what is expected of you.

Order. By being in control of what is expected of you, you can change the sequence (order) to your advantage.

Structure. You compare what is expected of you with what you want. The differences (structure) between the two show you where you can reverse one and produce change.

Relation. You compare the similarities (relation) between the way you have acted previously and the way you are expected to act in the present situation. Now you can reverse these to reach your solution.

Example. A Michigan bank attempted to use reversal to get new savings accounts. Instead of the toasters, dishes, briefcases, etc., that other banks offer, they decided to give away that very attractive item—money. They advertised that they would give 5 dollars to anyone who came in and opened an account and brought along the coupon at the bottom of the ad. One woman noticed that this ad was different from the usual bank ad—caution had been abandoned. No minimum deposit was required and no limit on "one per customer" was set. So she collected thirty-six coupons and opened thirty-six accounts, depositing 1 dollar in each. The bank reluctantly paid her $180 and moved fast to plug the loopholes.

Note that the woman considered order. She observed the reversal, change between the usual premium and this one. She noted the difference (structure) between getting new customers and getting new accounts. She saw the similarity (relation) between the traditional ad and the new one—both gave something to get something. She used that knowledge to her advantage.

DISASSOCIATION

This is a particularly available strategy for thinking creatively. You disassociate from the methods and solutions that have always worked for you, and try a new approach, even with a problem for which you already have a fairly satisfactory answer.

Order. By changing associations you see a sequence of changes (order) that have taken place or might take place in the future. You then can be better able to observe and compare the social, political, and other consequences of your original position.

Structure. By looking at the problem in a detached manner, different ways to solve it can become apparent.

Relation. You see the similarity in the differences between your present and a proposed approach. You discard the undesirable elements, thus creating a new, different and hopefully better position.

Example. In 1876, Alexander Graham Bell invented the telephone. Four years later, although his previous invention was becoming a commercial success, Bell obtained a patent for the photophone. Photographs of city streets from that era show a compelling reason for the seeming redundancy: telephone poles and masses of overhead wires were an unsightly blight. Instead of electric current in the new patent, he substituted light. As Bell Laboatories describes it: "Sunlight was bounced from a reflector through a lens to a mechanism that vibrated in response to speech. This caused the light beam to vary in intensity. At the receiving end a selenium detector translated these variations into an electrical current to recreate speech through a telephone receiver."

Note that Bell considered order on several levels. Looking down from above he could see the need for change in the telephone that would create a better social environment. From below he could see that only one major change in the telephone was necessary—switching the method of transmission from electricity to light. The other changes were minor. He dealt with structure (difference) by realizing that while light and electricity acted much in the same way, minor adjustments in the transmitting apparatus had to be made. Relation may have started Bell thinking. The similarity between light and electricity, once noted, was the key to the invention of the photophone.

A postscript is in order. Very few places on earth have sunlight twenty-four hours a day, and none have it all year long. Electricity *is* available twenty-four hours a day. So Bell's invention never got off the ground. But future inventors found other uses.

FORBEARANCE

You put a desired solution on the back burner and wait for the inevitable changes that time produces. One might be favorable.

Order. Let change work for you. However, you must be alert to recognize when the change takes place. It is all very well to have the pot on the back burner, but you must know when the dish is done—not overdone or underdone, but done to perfection.

Structure. You consider not only the different alternatives that change makes available to you, but also how time changes the problem and the ways of thinking about it.

Relation. You consider the similarities (relation) between your old and possible new solution, then evaluate them. Time changes and makes new relations.

Example. Almost eighty years after Bell received his patent for the photophone, Bell Laboratories took a second look at the concept of using light waves to transmit sound. The problem of the unreliability of sunlight had been solved by the development and perfection of laser and fiber optics. Not only did laser beams provide a constant source of light, fiber could transmit it around obstacles (which the photophone could not do). But best of all an incredible number of messages could be transmitted simultaneously over long distances. Perhaps, ironically, all of this was accomplished by using glass *wires* to carry the beams—the very thing that Bell had attempted to eliminate.

Note that the scientists at Bell Laboratories of course considered order when they turned to the laser—a change that time had wrought. But less obvious was the fact that the passage of time had eliminated the need for telephone poles and overhead wires. Differences (structure) were carefully analyzed. Some conclusions seem quite obvious, but one, perhaps less obvious, was recognition that with the change of time the nature of the problem also changed. In the old days telephones were few and far between. Today there is a great demand for more efficient transmission of multiple messages. Similarities (relation) were carefully weighed. For example, both the old and new solutions took into account the people's desire and need to communicate, the equipment available at the time, and so on. Time alone provides many useful alternatives.

FAIT ACCOMPLI

You impose your solution and let others have the burden of returning to the former status quo.

Order. Since this strategy can easily backfire, careful consideration of order is essential. Any change you contemplate must be carefully weighed. Do you have the ability to put it into effect and keep it in effect? Is the change too little or too late?

Structure. You ask yourself in what way a difference can make a difference. Will the change be enough to solve your problem? Will it produce new opposition too difficult to handle?

Relation. You ask if there are alternative solutions that offer similar results but use less risky strategies. This is important when you try a fait accompli. You should try to have a backup position.

Example. When Fiorello La Guardia was mayor of New York City in the 1930's, one man completely controlled the market in miniature artichokes, prized by members of the Italian community. To end this million-dollar racket, La Guardia, with typical flamboyance, appeared early one morning with a police escort and buglers, carrying a large proclamation. He climbed up on a truck bed, unrolled the proclamation, and read it to the assembled crowd. Under an ancient law, the mayor said, he had the right to ban the distribution of food in the city if an emergency should arise. There was now such an emergency, hence no artichoke would be sold in the city from that date.

Note the use of order: the mayor needed and produced change by studying the availability of and using his official powers. Structure was considered. He saw the difference (structure) between the helpless attitude of previous mayors and the use of a fait accompli to produce a significant change. Similarities (relation) were considered. Whether the "artichoke king" controlled the market or the mayor did, the law of supply and demand had been superseded.

One final detail: La Guardia had secretly sent an official to Washington to get the Department of Agriculture to revoke the racketeer's license to sell artichokes. The proclamation had only served to direct public attention to a serious problem.

BRACKETING

If you do not know where to look for your creative strategy, you may adopt a strategy familiar to World War I artillery-men—bracketing. You deliberately shoot over the target, then short of it. After calculation of the distance between the misses, you correct aim and are right on the target.

Order. When you change your aim, the time and place of the target become apparent. Your bracketing strategy, hope-fully, reveals your target's position.

Structure. By bracketing you are able to see the limitations imposed upon you by the rules and the problem. Does the structure you perceive yield an "on-target" solution or must you adjust your sights?

Relation. You see the similarity (relation) between your past and current positions. What adjustments must be made?

Example. An ailing pensioner, Signora Giuseppa Delogu of Sardinia, found herself the unwilling target of the bureau-cratic mind. The state electricity board sent her a bill for one lira (less than one eighth of a penny). A board spokesman explained: "The law requires we collect all sums due, however small. To clear this matter from our books will cost us several hundred lire." The local social security office saw a different problem. It was willing to pay the lady's electric bill, but pointed out that the five lire coin is Italy's smallest. Then, having shot over and under the target, the social security office offered a creative solution. "We will pay the bill with a five-lire coin—but we will be wanting our four-lire change."

Note that order is considered. The local office by bracketing the problem has learned its true dimensions. It can now propose a creative change (order). By understanding the difference (structure) between the unrealistic demand and actuality, it could fire right on the target. The similarity (relation) between the social security office's dilemma (no one-lira coin) and the potential dilemma of the electricity board provided the creative alternative solution.

BLANKETING

You use the shotgun approach. You cover the entire area with your fire and hope that you hit the target before the cease-fire comes.

Order. This strategy is unpredictable, change (order) is inevitable, but whether it will be advantageous to you or not depends on how selective you are in picking the target areas.

Structure. One important consideration is to cover as many of the different areas as possible.

Relation. Blanketing can produce creative thought *if* you are aware of the similarity (relation) to your past approaches where it worked before. Be sure to cover that area.

Example. Sometimes a bad example, a miss, is as instructive as a good one. Here is one of each.

New York City has a tow-away program for illegally parked cars. The cars are impounded and the owner has to pay a large towing fee and a parking fine to get the car back. One night someone got into the police car pound and slashed the tires of 49 of 76 tow trucks bedded down there. Towing operations of the city were virtually paralyzed the following day while the tires were repaired or replaced at a total cost of $5,000. The police later recalled that a Brooklyn man had been arrested in the wee hours of the night for trying to drive his car out of the pound without paying the fine. A Bowie knife had been found on the front seat of his car.

The man admitted to a newspaper reporter that he had done the wicked deed. (He later withdrew his confession.) He explained that he was angry because this had been the fourth time his car had been towed away, and each time "something" was broken. When he found his car at the pound there was the customary damage. Then he said, "These people have no compassion. They break your car and say the hell with it." So he slashed as many of the tires of the tow trucks as he could find before attempting to free his car.

If we give the man every benefit of the doubt, we might consider this as a creative irrational rampage. From the standpoint of time (order) he did gain a whole day during which the danger of being towed away again was minimal. Unfortunately he could not enjoy this triumph—he was in jail. He would, however, have to be given a flunking grade in structure, his rationality and relation. There the whole story is one of confusing differences and similarities. Where the man saw only similarities, a creative thinker would see differences, and vice versa. To point out a few examples: The slasher thought he was following an eye-for-an-eye procedure. You may damage my car and I'll damage yours.

A less emotional person would see it differently. Damaging 49 tow trucks is not the same as damaging one car. Because he could not see this difference (structure) he got into trouble and was carted away. If he had damaged one truck, it might have passed unnoticed, but 49 was excessive. He saw a relation between his right and the tow truck's attempts to deprive him of that right and damage his car. A creative person, and even a prudent one, would have looked for different ways (structure) to remedy his damages—perhaps a lawsuit against the city. A creative, more rational person would also note the relation not only between the "crimes" but also between the punishments. In other words, the creative person would view the whole thing in the larger context, not as isolated insufferable personal acts.

A better example of the use of blanketing took place in New York City also. Although it is difficult to deduce the motives of bureaucrats, this story could have been the result of a conscious use of blanketing. One day the Parks Commissioner announced that his department was "seriously considering" selling some of the city's 13 public golf courses to help close the city's budget gap. "We don't need 13 golf courses. They are a luxury and an under-utilized luxury." Use of them had steadily declined and running them cost the city $3 million and brought in only $1.8 million. He suggested, among other things, that the land might be sold to a major industry as the site for its headquarters building. Thus the sylvan nature of the property could be preserved.

To buttress his argument, the commissioner cited a study made for him by the United States Golf Association which concluded that a basic demographic change had occurred in the metropolitan area: the people most likely to play golf had moved to the Sun Belt.

Although the issue was unresolved early in 1979, letters to the editor and news developments indicated that the commissioner's blanketing approach had produced predictable responses: at least one neighborhood strongly opposed closing *their* golf course and were promised that it would stay open because it was more than paying its own way; environmentalists protested the selling of *any* park land and suggested other uses for it. None, however, opposed the elimination of at least some of the golf courses. Blanketing had produced a reevaluation of the proper use of public lands.

Note that the commissioner, of course, considered order (change) when he blanketed *all* the golf courses with the threat of closing them. He considered structure by sending up a trial balloon proposing a different use for the land. This proposal was predictably opposed by different groups, but the commissioner's eye was on the ball—eliminate costly and losing uses of park lands. He was content to let his opposition come up with creative alternatives. He noted relation: after all, no park land is expected to make a profit. However, he returned to structure. The golf courses were different from, say, Central Park. The park was for everyone, the golf courses for the "elite," and a vanishing elite at that.

ASSOCIATION

You link certain characteristics, attitudes and actions with those of an outstanding event or influential person.

Order. You change time and place so you can link other alternatives for your problem.

Structure. You might look for "blind spots" in the attitudes of the person you want to emulate to discover the difference (structure) between your attitude and his/hers. This can offer you a possible change.

Relation. You search and use the similarity between the other person's thoughts (and perhaps prejudices) and your own needs.

Example. Thomas A. Edison made the first successful light bulb. However, he was not interested merely in light bulbs. He wanted to establish a complete system from generators to meters to lamps.

His system was based on the use of direct current (DC). Soon, George Westinghouse established his own electric company to compete with Edison. He bought the patents of Nikola Tesla, who had worked briefly for Edison, had quarreled with him, and had picked up his patents and left. *His* system was based on alternating current (AC). The struggle between the two companies became increasingly bitter, and until his dying day Edison insisted on the superiority of DC current.

He even sponsored public demonstrations to "prove" that AC current was more dangerous than DC. (Actually, DC is slightly more dangerous.)

Edison and Westinghouse both became intense partisans of their systems. As *The New York Times* said in an article celebrating the 100th anniversary of a practical light bulb, "New York State penal reformers seeking a humane substitute for hanging were so impressed by his (Edison's) contentions, that they commissioned the world's first electric chair, powered by three Westinghouse AC generators."

Let's not pursue this grisly tale further. Note that structure, order and relation are all there, and the reformers certainly used association in inventing their "humane" solution. George Westinghouse, on the other hand, felt himself a victim of association. He tried in vain to prevent the use of *his* generators to execute the first victim of the electric chair in 1890. After witnessing the first electric chair execution, he said, "They could have done it better with an ax."

LIMITS

You say, "This far and no further," limits in space and time. ("Pay now or pay a penalty.") With people, "If you deal with them, I won't do business with you."

Order. Limit a deal by changing time and place. You can change them to discover new dimensions of your problem. Look for ways to restructure your possible new solutions to fit the limits you have set, thus producing change (order).

Structure. A limit has the ability to bring problems into focus, make things real. As Samuel Johnson said: "Depend on it, sir, when a man knows he is to be hanged in a fortnight, it concentrates his mind wonderfully." In such an atmosphere, alternatives are not only possible but necessary.

Relation. Certain aspects of the old and new solutions will be similar. Limits should be used in areas where your change is likely to produce a creative solution, a better result.

Example. Giacomo Puccini was a descendant of four generations of Puccinis who had occupied the lifetime post of organist and choirmaster at the Cathedral of San Martino in Lucca. Everyone assumed that Giacomo would follow in their footsteps. When his father died, the six-year-old boy was assigned to the post "as soon as the said Signor Giacomo is able to discharge such duties." He was rather unpromising material: lazy, a poor student, displaying only average talent in musical composition, and with a complete aversion to the organ. However, at age fourteen he began to play the organ at the cathedral. He also demonstrated a certain precocity by becoming a chain smoker of cigars and cigarettes at about this time.

To help support this habit, he later told a friend, he would steal the smaller, concealed organ pipes and sell them. His problem: how to cover up the theft. His solution: he made appropriate changes in the harmony of whatever he played to avoid the missing notes and play only those pipes that remained. Who knows? Perhaps this early challenge helped him on the road to becoming a master composer.

Note that order was certainly in evidence in the harmonic changes. Differences (structure) were obligatory to accommodate the limited choices of notes. Relation played its part. Every aspect of the new music had to be similar to the old—except for the harmony. There was, as we can appreciate, a natural limit to the pipes he could steal.

CROSSROADS

You assemble and examine many options before deciding which path will be traveled to provide you with a creative solution.

Order. You test many alternatives to see which one will bring constructive change. Often this can be the shortest and most direct path, always considering both distance and time.

Structure. Viewing your problem down different roads will give a clearer idea of the structures of the problem and provide you with alternative approaches to solving it.

Relation. You study similarities (relation) in the process you are dealing with. This can lead you to a direct path for solving your problem. Consider, have you been down that path before?

Example. Early in 1979 a strange-looking device was hoisted to the roof of a building housing New York University's Department of Applied Science. It was a prototype of the Lebost Wind Turbine. If its exterior looked like a standard silo cover, that was because it *was.* It was designed to harness the power of wind and convert it into useful energy. At the same time, the Department of Energy was developing giant wind machines resembling the old-fashioned windmill but with blades the length of a football field. They were expected to be capable of producing large amounts of electricity.

The Lebost wind machine is very different from these monsters. First, its blades (structure), which are only twenty-one feet across, spin on an upright shaft. Then, instead of relying on the free-flowing thrust of the wind, the turbine's structural elements are used to channel and concentrate the wind's power (relation). Barry A. Lebost, the inventor, claimed that his blades capture two to three times as much power from the wind as would conventional windmill blades of similar size. The final difference was that the turbine did not produce electricity, it produced heat. The four blades moved relatively slowly, so it was not very efficient as a generator of electricity. However, because all blades were engaged at the same time, they had considerably more torque than the conventional wind machine. This made them ideal for turning friction devices that could convert mechanical energy into heat (order).

Note that whether the turbine will prove to be practical or not remains to be seen. However, it is a fine example of the use of crossroads strategy to bring structure, order and relation to bear on finding a creative solution. One of Mr. Lebost's comments is especially interesting. After noting that fully one third of the United States' energy consumption goes into the production of heat, he said: "Since the wind happens to be very close to heat itself—it was created by heat—it is less of a conversion to bring it back to heat than to turn it into 60-cycle electricity."

SURPRISE

You suddenly shift your approach to your problem and attempt a solution in this new area.

Order. Although you retain your original objective or motive, you shift and adopt the point of view of the person(s) you are trying to influence. You can then discover what the person likes and also what he does not like. You change approach (order) and you can achieve your objective by playing up what the person does *not* like.

Structure. Changing viewpoints suddenly can open different routes to reach your goal.

Relation. Suddenly stop offering differences. Make your point of view (or objective) compatible with the other person's. This will point up similarities (relation) that all sides can preserve while you reach your creative solution.

Example. Roger Starr, reminiscing about his World War II experiences in *The New York Times,* told this story:

> Recent editorials and letters urging the study of the Chinese language have my fervent support, based on six months I spent as an Army second lieutenant in Asia in World War II, editing an ostensibly official Japanese Army Chinese-language newspaper. The journal's true publisher was my employer, the Office of Strategic Services, which arranged to distribute it to civilians in occupied China. I managed my share of this complex feat despite the fact that I knew no word of Chinese or Japanese. The purpose of the O.S.S. "Japanese Army" paper was subversive. Our job was to achieve the maximum possible number of intercultural *faux pas* per column inch. We were to mangle the Chinese language in ways peculiarly natural to Japanese outlanders, and especially vexing to Chinese "patriots." He had to rely on "two brilliant Chinese journalists, exiles from occupied Shanghai."

Note the use of order: the whole caper was based on not only preserving the American point of view but adopting the Chinese with its antipathy to the Japanese as invaders and also cultural "barbarians." Differences (structure) were duly noted in emphasizing the "funny accent" of the Japanese. The similarity (relation) between the American and Chinese desire to drive the Japanese out was played up in the ensuing deception.

Mr. Starr's problem, however, was that since he did not know Chinese or Japanese he had no way of knowing whether the journalists "were writing flawless Chinese, winning the hearts of the conquered people instead of stirring them to bloody rebellion." In other words, because of an educational deficiency he could not tell the difference (structure) between "flawless" Chinese and that written by the Japanese conquerors. The surprise was that he tried it at all or that he would want to write about it.

PARTICIPATION

You combine your thoughts with those interested in dealing with your problem. Ideally, the resulting approach will combine the strengths of both.

Order. You are prepared to change (order) your thinking to coincide with the aims and direction of the person you want to join you. You can add your strengths to those of the other person.

Structure. By contrasting your thinking with those of another person, you see the differences (structure) between your strengths and his/hers.

Relation. By comparing the other person's thinking with your own, you discover the similarities (relation) in aims in both points of view. You help them emphasize those factors that suit your purposes.

Example. A Brooklyn man, helping out a friend, changed an eight-foot fluorescent tube for him. He then left for home taking the used tube with him. Somehow, he could not find an appropriate place to dispose of the tube. It was still with him when he got on the subway. After he stood holding the tube, vertically, for several stops, he was joined by three other men who also held on to the tube which externally resembles a subway car holding pole. So the man quietly disengaged himself and walked to the other end of the subway car.

Note that change (order) was important in finding the "right atmosphere" to solve the problem. Differences (structure) were apparent in the man's knowledge that this was a fluorescent tube while his fellow passengers thought it was just another pole to hold on to. Relation (similarity) separated the traditionalists from the innovator.

RANDOMIZING

You are faced with an intractable, traditional idea that interferes with your attempts to reach a creative solution. You select at random a number of tentative creative approaches that may help you. You might even toss a coin to determine your actions. However, you are creative in the selection of your choice. After all, even in tossing a coin you have decided on that method of pure choice, not astrology or any other such way to predict the future.

Order. Your selection here is pure chance for the sake of pure chance.

Structure. Randomizing insures that you will see differences (structure). You deliberately set out to find new ways that are in variance with the traditional one.

Relation. Similarities of solutions can allow you to use randomizing to determine a promising path to follow.

Example. After-the-fact analysis of the thinking of geniuses is risky on one level but instructive on another. Einstein's theory of special relativity is a case in point. Probably nobody could accurately recreate the process he used. However, any creative person can use randomizing to stimulate thought or to reach a solution that would bear a remote but nonetheless real resemblance to an element in Einstein's theory.

The theory was a bold attack on the system of mechanics formulated by Sir Isaac Newton. Two of Newton's basic assumptions were that time and distance are absolute and remain universally the same. Einstein argued that both concepts were wrong. Both depend on the relative motion of observers (point of view). For example, he presented this thought experiment: an observer standing near a railroad track sees two bolts of lightning, one from the west, the other from the east, strike the tracks simultaneously. At the same time, a train moving at high speed from east to west passes directly in front of him. An observer on the train would not think the bolts struck simultaneously because he is moving away from the bolt in the west so the light takes a longer time to reach him, and toward the bolt in the east so it appears to come sooner. Under different circumstances, of course, the passenger might conclude that the bolts struck simultaneously while the stationary observer would see a time gap between them.

Note that Einstein carefully considered order by stating that change in time and place can affect the way we see things. He considered structure (difference) in observing that differing points of view were dependent on relative motion. He used relation to show that both observers had similar faculties and only relative motion made them see things differently where there was similarity.

RANDOM SAMPLE

You have a fairly clear idea of the direction you should take to reach a solution. Therefore, you do not need to randomize completely. Instead, you select a possible solution at random within the boundaries you have decided on. This will help you decide on a more appropriate solution.

Order. You have deliberately limited your options for change (order) and can therefore be highly selective in choosing the solution (change) that best fits your purpose.

Structure. Your selection will depend on the differing results you will get from the randomly selected solutions. If your samples are not broad enough, you may very well be misled to choose an inappropriate solution.

Relation. You also must be aware of the similarities (relation) between your approaches, i.e., all must lead to the same goal. Then you can choose the one that gets you there most expeditiously. You have selected from the selection.

Example. As every schoolboy is taught, Samuel Colt is credited with being one of the founders of modern technology. He was one of the first to manufacture products with interchangeable parts. His first success came at the outbreak of the Mexican War, when the federal governmental placed an order for one thousand of his soon-to-be-famous revolvers.

Note that Colt considered order by using the random sample strategy. He of course wanted to make the revolvers in the most efficient manner possible, and interchangeable parts were the answer. He considered structure by evaluating the different ways he could manufacture revolvers and choosing the "best" one. He used relation by seeing similarity. Instead of "seeing" one thousand individual revolvers, he "saw" *the* Colt revolver, each indistinguishable from any other Colt revolver.

Alas, it now appears that what every schoolboy believes is incorrect. Apparently, Colt's claim to fame was accepted because Colt himself said it was so. In the February, 1979, issue of *Scientific American*, an article by Robert A. Howard revealed the sad truth. The writer, a gun collector and museum curator, told how he also used the random sample technique to get at the truth. He asked several gun collectors to disassemble their Colt revolvers. Randomly selected parts could not be put together to produce an effective gun. The parts were *not* uniform. Apparently, Colt workers picked over machine-made parts until they came up with sets that fit together fairly well. "Fine tuning" was accomplished by hand filing. Even worse, he discovered that Colt to this day still cannot make revolvers with fully interchangeable parts.

Colt apparently had a firm grasp of order—he knew that such a change was desirable. However, he had to compromise on structure and relation. No available machinery could produce perfectly identical parts, and the difference made a difference. He was also unable to make a real change in relation. All Colt revolvers were similar, but they were not the same.

SALAMI

You are faced with a hydra-headed problem. Every time you cut off one head, two grow in its place. Hercules solved the problem by *burning* off eight of the heads and burying the ninth, immortal one under a huge rock. The salami strategy is similar. You tackle the problem by slicing off a piece at a time until you have the whole thing.

Order. Since every slice you take will produce a change, you are of course concerned with order. However, in slicing the salami you must decide on the amount, size and time of each slice to achieve the end result you desire, just as Hercules used fire instead of a sword to gain his.

Structure. You must study the different possible methods to reach the one that serves your purpose best. Each new slice makes a difference.

Relation. You must be very conscious of the similarities in the material you are working on, asking how a repeat of similarity can help you reach your goal.

Example. Dr. Elvin Charles Stakman was a pioneering plant pathologist and an authority on the diseases of wheat and other food crops. One of his many accomplishments was to persuade the Rockefeller Foundation to initiate a major program to improve crop yields in developing nations. The result was the Green Revolution that dramatically increased the food production throughout the world.

Perhaps his greatest contribution was a result of his study of wheat-stem rust, a fungal disease that periodically destroyed wheat crops throughout the world. A *New York Times* article explained: "Dr. Stakman discovered wheat rust was not a single, unchanging entity. Instead, he found, it was constantly evolving and spawning new strains that could infect plants that were resistant to other strains of rust."

Building on Dr. Stakman's work, wheat scientists now have a global network of specialists trained to detect new strains of wheat rust before they can spread. As a result, plant breeders can develop strains of wheat with appropriate resistance and get them into farmers' fields before the new rust spreads.

The whole process changed with each new phase.

Note that Dr. Stakman was very conscious of order (change) in discovering that rusts could mutate. This, of course, led to (or resulted from) a study of structure (differences). Relation also got its due. No matter what their differences, all rusts could be controlled by plant breeders using similar methods to produce disease-resistant plants. These are only examples of his use of structure, order, and relation to solve this hydra-headed problem. As Dr. Stakman once said, "We need to remember that science dedicates itself to the discovery, organization and humanization of truth." This philosophy is equally valid for any creative thinker, whatever his field.

FEINTING

You divert attention by pretending to attack a problem while you ready a blow at a different, vital center.

Order. Change is implicit in this strategy. You feint when you change your apparent direction to hit the real target. For example, Mayor Frank Rizzo of Philadelphia won two terms without difficulty, but was finally put out of office when he tried to remove the restriction against more than two terms from the city charter. His opponents seemed to be attacking a charter change. Actually they were effectively removing the mayor from office.

Structure. You note the difference between your apparent and your real target. After all, you want to attack a weak point, not a strong one.

Relation. Paradoxically, consistency is essential when you use this strategy. You must not waiver in your overall objective of solving the problem or you yourself will be diverted from your goal.

Example. In an article in *Keynote* (published by radio station WNCN, New York), Dale Harris wonders which of Benjamin Britten's operas will survive. With one exception, he does not think they will. Pointing out that *Billy Budd* demonstrates Britten's "uncanny instinct for the stage" he mentions "the perfect naturalness with which he seized upon language" (relation), "his knowledge of the human voice's expressive power" (order), "his choice of precisely the right orchestral timbre to objectify his vocal ideas and convert them into the stuff of musical drama" (structure). This, of course, meets our definition of creativity, but it is not an example of feinting. That comes later in the article and points up the peril of using this strategy unwisely.

Time after time, Harris says, Britten in other operas introduces characters and themes that set the stage beautifully, then when he should build to a smashing climax he does not do it. "By allowing his protagonist to ramble on in a manner dangerously close to musical incoherence and then failing to set Balstrode's lines to music, Britten—or so it seems to me—had abandoned music drama for melodrama, had denied himself, for reasons I could not fathom, access to the infinite resources of musical expressivity." In other words, Britten's fatal flaw was in feinting and then forgetting his real target—a dramatic completion of the opera. He hits with all his musical force in the beginning and uses his weakest devices at the end.

Note that he has failed to give structure, order and relation their proper places. After all, unless the end is different from the beginning and better, there is no drama. The characters must grow (change), yet they must be consistent throughout.

A more happy example is a favorite story of Supreme

Court Justice William O. Douglas. On a plane flight the going got very rough and apprehension among the passengers built. Finally a little old lady suggested that the justice "do something religious." He obliged. He took up a collection. This is feinting at its best. The lady expected a prayer. Instead, Douglas hit at the real problem: calming the passengers.

EXERCISE

Life constantly presents us with unexpected experiences.
How would you have acted creatively?

A Gypsy Story

A minor poet once wrote: "There is something in October
sets the gypsy blood astir." In one case, as reported by *The
Washington Post* (February 2, 1980), the mood carried over
into the following month as the following case study shows.
Under a headline "I've Been Robbed Before but This Was
More Traumatic," Chip Brown tells of the experience en-
dured by John Allen, manager of a supermarket in Glen-
mont.

On the afternoon of Nov. 8, 1979, a three-car caravan of
gypsies showed up at Allen's store. According to police
accounts:

While the bulk of the gypsy caravan lingered out in the
parking lot, four women entered the supermarket. A 22-year-
old gypsy climbed up a cigar rack into the overhead office
where $250 was padlocked in a strong box. Her three com-
panions stayed nearby. Allen, who had been in aisle four re-
designing a display of disposable diapers, heard a commotion
coming from the office. As he ran towards the office, the three
advanced to meet him. They were wearing long, black and
green silk skirts, loose blouses and turquoise rings. One
grabbed Allen's arm, another put her shawl in front of his
face. During the ensuing scuffle, the cigar-rack climber
whisked her dress over her head, and according to court papers, "revealed her genital area in an apparent attempt to
cause further commotion." As Allen observed later: "She
picked up her dress and didn't have anything on. You don't
see things like that every day in a grocery store." Undaunted,
Allen tried to push her against the dog food, but "she was
rather heavy." Another gypsy "pulled the top of her clothes
up exposing her breasts and causing considerable disruption
to the operation of the store and considerable anguish."

Store employees finally corralled the four and in poured twenty-five young gypsies, one carrying a baby which he handed to one of the captive women who promptly began to breast-feed it. Allen said, "We thought they had money from the cash box. We thought they were trying to slip it into the baby's diaper." Then a 15-year-old gypsy bit Allen's right wrist which punctured the skin. "When she bit me," Allen said, "I wanted to punch her lights out, but I didn't want to hit a woman, even though it would have released a lot of tension."

All of this took ten minutes to happen. Seven squad cars and four plainclothes officers spent eight hours subduing the four women and booking them. They posted a $6,000 bond with money they fished out of a car trunk and disappeared from the Washington scene.

Calling the police is perhaps effective but it isn't a creative solution to the problem. What would you have done?

V

Expanding Former Methods Used to Understand Creativity

The method of our time is to use not a single but multiple models for exploration—the technique of the suspended judgment is the discovery of the Twentieth Century as the technique of invention was the discovery of the Nineteenth.

Marshall McLuhan, *The Medium Is the Message*

16

The Interdisciplinary Analogue Laboratory with Creative Thinking Skills

The fusion of knowledge is the most creative act of the human mind.

—Elwood Murray

The next several chapters are brief outlines of former methods that are being used to help individuals become more creative. Each method can be enlarged and made more meaningful throughout by use of the creative thinking skills.

In the last half of the twentieth century, students of General Semantics have used various techniques to assist them in evaluating their lives and environments. In doing so they have enhanced their insights and concern to be creative. The Interdisciplinary Analogue Laboratory, pioneered by Elwood Murray, a leader in general semantics, is a fine illustration. The laboratory was designed to stimulate creative ideas through group participation. Small groups containing members with different background experiences are formed. To obtain a fusion of knowledge, specialists from various disciplines, as in arts and sciences, are brought together. They discuss the underlying structural similarities in a creative manner. These "hidden likenesses" are revealed by means of analogy. According to Professor Murray: "Analogy, by definition, concerns the likeness between two things or one thing to or with another." Although Murray also emphasizes structure (differences) in his concepts, we can easily identify relations as a distinguishing feature stressed in the Analogue

Laboratory. Again, "In biology, analogy consists of correspondence in function between organs or parts of different structures and organs." (Here relation predominates.) "In general semantics . . . analogy refers to the isomorphism—the similarities between and among structures." The end result is that we are more aware of our own problem and solutions through analogies with others.

Murray's classification of analogies which are used within the laboratories by the groups can be stated and compared with Embler's three languages:

1. *Literal analogy*—comparison between and among things in the same category. Two cars of the same model and make is one example. (This is relation and structure.)

2. *Figurative analogy*—comparison between and among things in different categories. In *Metaphor and Meaning*, Embler provides an interesting example: the metaphors of communication theory, which indicate the way the human nervous system is likened to devices of modern technology. "Forty years ago . . . lecturers in psychology spoke of 'neural patterns' and listeners visualized intricate networks of roadways . . . some wide and well traveled (the old thoughts and reflexes), and some less well traveled and wanting wear (new thoughts and delayed reactions). A generation later, the nervous system was likened to a complex telephonic organization in which messages are sent out through central exchanges over the 'wires' of the system to all areas of the organism. Recently, the telephone metaphor has been supplanted by an electronic metaphor. Today, as a complex of routes or wires conveying messages, the nervous system is all but abolished in favour of biochemical energy exchanges." (This is illustrative of structure and relation.)

Metaphor—a condensation of figurative analogy, which is an essence of literature (see Chapter 11).

The Analogue Laboratory technique specifies that analogies are concerned not so much with the superficial comparisons of things as: "If you've seen one slum, you've seen them all." This does not even qualify as a valid analogy. Analogy deals rather with two or more attributes, circumstances or effects. When Shakespeare said, "All the world's a stage," he concentrates on the attributes shared by "men and women" and "players." There is not a great stage manager "up there" or other distracting analogy. The entire passage is vivid and to the point. It and other creative analogies deal with "a form of inference in which it is reasoned that, if two or more things agree with one another in one or more respects, they will probably agree in other respects." The aspects that are being compared, however, must be only of basic, intrinsic parts. (The structures must correspond in certain essential ways.) The structures the group members discuss must be causally, not casually, related. (There must be an awareness of similar, underlying orders.) Furthermore, the relationships must be "qualitative as well as quantitative." (The relationships established must seem valid and apt.)

To make an Analogue Laboratory function more effectively, participants must pay sufficient attention to the levels of their abstraction and have awareness of points of view. There must first be a common meeting ground since "no analogy is generated unless the things to be compared are reduced sufficiently to their operational and relational levels of existence." If this should seem like a minor, unimportant "rule," consider the countless metaphors invented by poets and later by writers of cosmetics ads to describe the beauty, softness, and perfection of a woman's skin. Then turn to Swift's *Gulliver's Travels* and read his gross description of human skin as seen through the eyes of a person infinitely smaller than the subject. This is a microscopic, objectionable view imposed on something that macroscopically seems quite beautiful. The results here are devastating. However, when statements are, for example, reduced to their macroscopic levels of sensory observation and description, then the participants are able to understand and check on the others' observations.

What exactly does the Analogue Laboratory try to accomplish? *First,* to develop an instrument for "making discoveries as to the nature of the symbolizing and communication process—including rational, critical, and creative thinking." Clues derived from analogy may then be formulated into hypotheses for thinking. Analogy thus becomes the creative spark that stimulates constructive (and even practical) thinking. *Second,* "to ascertain some of the physical connections at the operational levels among our knowledges . . . viewed relationally and operationally, there is unity and wholeness in the universe of which man is part. Man as a communicator will perhaps forever face the challenge of filling in the gaps and vacuums in his own comprehensions concerning these (relational) structures, the ever increasing number with which he must cope to survive."

One can appreciate by this process that, before this laboratory will fully work, one should be aware of the creative thinking skills, know the level and the use of each and every structure, order and relation term (remembering here again, the individual's attention, point of view, is most often riveted on and limited to one interest only.)

The Analogue Laboratory becomes a most useful tool in developing more alternative thinking when used with a working knowledge of the creative thinking skills.

EXERCISE

Working of an Analogue Laboratory

A. Go to assigned groups.
   1. Groups contain different disciplines.
   2. Everyone is given an opportunity to speak.
   3. Feedback chairperson is appointed.

B. Examine your discipline and choose a structure that you use on the lowest level thinkable (e.g., dancer chooses rhythms).
   1. Each member describes to his or her group his or her structure after all have reported.
   2. Each member then discusses the other person's structure in relation to what they do.
      a. How do they use structures?
      b. Relations between structures.

C. After a full discussion by groups:
   1. Did your point of view of your structure change in any way?
   2. Could you have chosen a more basic level for your structure?
   3. Did any specific person or discipline effect your point of view of your structure?

D. Feedback chairperson will be prepared to summarize the discussion results.
   1. Each participant keeps a list of interpretations of the structures of other participants.

17

Brainstorming with Creative Thinking Skills

A moratorium is placed on evaluation until all ideas of the group are in.

—A. F. Osborne

In 1941, A.F. Osborne originated brainstorming. It was one of the many different attempts that have been made to stimulate an individual's creativity. The advertising profession, of which he was a member, used it extensively. This experience involves a group in which various ideas are expressed and critical judgment and evaluation are deferred until a later period. It is hoped that an uninhibiting environment will produce a ping-pong effect among the participants and help them bring new thoughts out of their preconscious imagination. The method used is to have a group of up to twelve discuss a specific problem. One of the members serves as a secretary, and records the remarks and suggestions that are made. Everyone withholds any judgment or evaluation of the suggestions or statements or names that have come up. After the session is over, the decision-maker goes through the various statements recorded by the secretary and uses what he determines is appropriate, relevant and practical.

It is hoped that this group method will increase the collective quality of thinking and good ideas. Whether this has any effect upon the participants in their subsequent approach to their individual problems has not been proven. At least there have been no reports of experiments designed to test increased creativity in the participants. However, any experience which releases an individual from preconceived notions that creativity is something that he is either born with or not is beneficial. Such approaches permit the individual thereafter to seek alternative ways of finding different solutions. Attention to creativity, knowledge of its existence, and procedures which are designed to increase it cannot help but enrich our lives.

Brainstorming would seem to have the effect of breaking down an individual's rigid categories by opening him to the insights and the fantasies of other persons while dealing with the same problem. They can be seeing the problem differently from his structural, ordered and relational point of view. Brainstorming does not, however, deal with or consider how each person's approach to the problem is different in point of view, and in level, with a different combination and variation of structure, order and relation. This prevents the group from realizing its full potential. In some of these respects, participation of the Interdisciplinary Analogue Laboratory experience gives greater insights than brainstorming.

It is here suggested that improvements can be made in brainstorming. This would consist of asking the group first to think of different structuring of the problem, then the relation possibilities, then order, reserving judgment of all as to whether they conform to the others' concepts or not. After the meeting, the suggestions would be examined by the group in the critical manner that would permit the members to see the points of view and the levels that each individual might be working on (e.g., whether they are looking at the problem in a macro manner or a micro manner). Then another meeting would utilize all that was discussed. As with the other methods, relating brainstorming to the creative thinking skills—structure, order, relation, level and point of view adds new dimensions.

Three basic rules for brainstorming are worth reviewing.

They have a relevance for many techniques that deal with creativity:

1. All ideas, regardless of their quality, are desired.

2. Ping-ponging and hitchhiking ideas as well as modifying and combining them with previously stated ideas are encouraged.

3. Criticism, verbally or nonverbally, is initially not allowed. It is particularly important that new ideas, often vague and imprecise, not be evaluated. *Constructive* criticism should be reserved for a later time (whether it is by you or others.)

18

Synectics with Creative Thinking Skills

Another technique for group problem-solving is synectics. It is somewhat like, but not as broad in scope as, the Interdisciplinary Analogue Laboratory. Collective attempts are made to investigate background information, boil down problems to their basics and solve problems by looking for natural analogies. A group is composed of carefully selected individuals and an experienced leader.

Its creator, William J. J. Gordon, defines synectics as meaning "the joining together of different and apparently irrelevant elements." ° Also, like the Analogue Laboratory, these creative insights are ultimately expected to be tested and put to constructive use. Although the individual process in the creative enterprise enjoys an "indirect analogy in group process," Gordon feels that "a synectics group can compress into a few hours the kind of semiconscious mental activity which might take months of incubation for a single person." Again, as was suggested in brainstorming and other methods, if the individual participants were first given an insight into the creative skills by understanding structure, order, relation, level and point of view, they would be able to magnify their individual potential and add to group ac-

° *Synectics,* Harper & Row, 1961.

tivities. In the first and last place, it is the individual who is creative.

Synectics avoids one of the criticisms of brainstorming: that it begins with answers. Synectics examines problem definition in detail. It attempts to solve problems creatively by "making the strange familiar and the familiar strange," using four mechanisms, "each metaphorical in character:"

1. Personal Analogy

2. Direct Analogy

3. Symbolic Analogy

4. Fantasy Analogy

Personal analogy involves identifying oneself with an object or process. It helps change one's point of view and also the level at which one may be seeing the problem. As mentioned earlier, Piaget learned that young children find it difficult, if not impossible, to see things from another's point of view. (It is when one thinks and reacts on an open-minded adult level that personal analogies can become meaningful.) Stated simply, a personal analogy can be the result of asking the question, "What would it feel like to be something entirely different (a molecule, a tin cup, or anything)?" This is a very difficult process and requires both practice and the suspension of logical or critical analysis. It can otherwise easily degenerate into one of several immature patterns of thought and emotion such as fantasizing ("What would I do if I were rich and famous?") or personification (hitting an inanimate object because it "hurt" or "frustrated" you). There is a difference between a teenager trying to imagine herself old and worn and an old, experienced and fulfilled woman knowing some of the feelings of the teenager. (This is again where creative skills of using structure, order and relation, level and point of view minimize these problems.)

Direct analogy involves the ability to see a previously un-recognized correspondence (relation) between two different objects or processes (structures). The popular story of Isaac Newton and the falling apple is a classic example of the direct analogy, which has as its core the question: "If X works in a certain desirable way, why can't Y work in a similar manner?" We are trained to "see" how X and Y differ. That is how we tell them apart. (If we do not immediately see similarities, we do not know how to look for them, how to change levels and point of view. Usually we are content with "all men are alike" kind of generality. Thus we find it difficult to "make the strange familiar" by use of direct analogy.)

Symbolic analogy "uses objective and impersonal images to describe the problem." It is compressed, concise and complete. Any good poetic metaphor can serve as an example. Symbolic analogies are products of the subconscious mind and, like the Greek goddess Athena, spring full grown (from Zeus' brow, or your own). If consciously patched together out of logical thoughts, they are somewhat contrived and virtually useless. The groundwork for the "intuitive leap" that produces them can, however, be carefully laid by the use of the five creative thinking skills.

Fantasy analogy requires a complete suspension (at least briefly) of self-consciousness, critical ideas and logical thought. Even the wildest ideas should not be excluded, as, for example, training insects to do mini-jobs. In fashioning a fantasy analogy, you will find that you have connected the world of the known with the world of the possible.

In synectics, the above specific applications are given to assist in the creative search.

Remember your subjective world is under your control. You can use your creative thinking to change points of view, levels, structures, orders and relations. Understanding allows you to use analogies creatively.

19

Dream Education

Change dreams toward maturity . . .
—Clare Stewart Flagg

If you are looking for new worlds to conquer, do not neglect the world of dreams. Kilton Stewart ° went beyond the conflicting theories of the meaning of dream symbols to study how human beings interact with dream symbols and with everyday happenings. His creative psychology is a study of the structural relationships between dream symbols and the event level. As a result of his work he was able to develop a theory leading to dream education. He believed that a person could achieve maturity on the subconscious level by discovering, confronting, outfacing and conquering his dream symbols. Through practice he could reorder (change) dream symbols to produce helpful images that eliminate nightmare effects and provide creative, positive and useful solutions to problems.

We too often remember only those dreams that leave a problem unresolved, an action incomplete, a terror unalleviated. It is as though we were duplicating on a subsconscious level our negative and noncreative mental patterns. We revert to childhood dream confusion and frustration. We do

---

° In numerous articles and *Pygmies and Dream Giants*, W. W. Norton, N.Y. 1954.

not manage our dreams, they manage us. According to Stewart this can be changed.

After all, dreams are our point of view. They deal with structure, order and relation on many levels as do our conscious thoughts. They can be changed and brought to maturity by a patient process of "learning the language" of symbols, of "thinking" in unfamiliar ways by the use of our creative thinking skills.

Clare Stewart Flagg, Kilton Stewart's widow, who carried on his work in the Stewart Foundation for Creative Psychology advises: "Change dreams toward maturity, complete, socialize and evaluate dreams through educating. Such education can help you remember dreams as well as possess and strengthen helpful images, and change harmful images. Socialize your dreams through supportive criticism. Dream to resolution and a productive result."

Most of us have sadly neglected the world of dreams, which occupies a substantial portion of our sleep. Dreams or stages of reverie, in time of relaxation or work, may yield a creative insight but only to the person who has consciously desired it and worked on and considered the problem. Learn to live positively and creatively in this dream world that has provided so many of the new solutions to problems for the talented geniuses and prophets.

Some examples of creativity as a result of dreams are:

Otto Louve's discovery of the chemical transmission of nerve impulses.

Dmitri Mendeleev's solution for the arrangement of the elements that came to him in a dream.

Kekulé's dream of a snake swallowing its own tail, giving the clue to the structure of benzene.

Samuel Taylor Coleridge's inspiration for the poem "Kubla Khan."

Robert Louis Stevenson's attributing his creativity to his

202 THE ART OF CREATIVE THINKING

dream time. *The Strange Case of Dr. Jekyll and Mr. Hyde* is a prime example.

Louis Agassiz, the naturalist, succeeded in locating a fossil through his dreams—but only after the third try.

In *The Dragons of Eden,* Carl Sagan observes:

> It may be that the left hemisphere [of the brain] is not entirely turned off at night but instead is performing tasks that make it inaccessible to consciousness; it is busily engaged in data dumping from the short-term memory buffer, determining what should survive into long-term storage.

You can have your share in discoveries that will change your life—and perhaps the lives of others.

EXERCISE

A Dream Diary

1. Keep a notebook or tape recorder for your dreams by the side of your bed.

2. Before going to sleep, direct yourself to dream.

3. Make a record of your dreams as soon as you wake—in the middle of the night or in the morning.

4. Analyze your dreams with reference to your symbolic life.

5. Did you ever request yourself while still dreaming to analyze the dream? This can prove interesting.

20

Altered States of Consciousness

The use of hypnosis to maximize creativity
"is in harmony with the future evolution of man"
                                          —Sir Julian Huxley

Altered states of consciousness—trance, drowsiness, sleep, meditation and drug intoxication are among those states most often studied—have long been associated with creativity. Once we realize the importance of point of view in the process, it is easy to see how this can be so. For example: "The meditation process produces alterations in the visual perception of sensory and formal properties of the object, and alterations in ego boundaries—all in the direction of fluidity and breakdown of the usual subject-object differentiation." °

In *Altered States of Consciousness*, Willis Harman, Robert McKim, Robert Mogar and James Fadiman list ten characteristics of the psychedelic experience that support creativity:

1. Increased access to unconscious data.

2. More fluent free association. Increased ability to play spontaneously with hypotheses, metaphors, paradox, transformations, relationships, etc.

° Charles T. Tarb, ed., *Altered States of Consciousness* (New York: Doubleday and Co., 1972).

3. Heightened ability for visual imagery and fantasy.

4. Relaxation and openness.

5. Sensory inputs more acutely perceived.

6. Heightened empathy with external processes, objects and people.

7. Aesthetic sensibility heightened.

8. Enhanced sense of truth, ability to see through false solutions and data.

9. Lessened inhibition, reduced tendency to render premature negative judgments.

10. Motivation may be heightened by suggestion and providing the right set.

These would indeed be valuable characteristics to have. In fact, probably all of them are necessary to some degree in the creative process. But is a drug-induced state the only way to acquire them? Of course not! With a conscientious intellectual effort to utilize creative thinking skills of structure, order and relation, level and point of view one can achieve the same objectives. The results, moreover, tend to be more consistently creative. In drug-induced states, according to many studies, creative performance may remain the same or even deteriorate. This is part of the bad news of the psychedelic experience. The same authors also list ten characteristics of the psychedelic experience that hinder creativity:

1. Capacity for logical thought process may be diminished.

2. Ability to consciously direct concentration may be reduced.

3. Inability to control imaginary and conceptual sequences.

4. Anxiety and agitation.

5. Outputs—verbal and visual communication abilities may be constricted.

6. Tendency to focus on "inner" problems of a personal nature.

7. The experience itself may be satisfying enough to reduce the need for creativity.

8. Tendency to become absorbed in hallucinations and illusions.

9. Finding the "best" solution may seem unimportant.

10. "This-worldly" tasks may seem trivial and hence motivation may be decreased.

Just as the desirable characteristics of a drug-induced state can be duplicated by other means, so can the undesirable ones be avoided with other means. Use this second list to make sure that your self-induced states of mind are not interfering with your creative potential.

VI

Life Uses of Your Creative Thinking Skills

If want is the mistress of invention
and necessity is the mother of invention,
isn't it time for Mr. Creativity
to stand up and be accounted for?

Gerard I. Nierenberg

21

Puzzle- and Riddle-Solving with Creative Thinking Skills

> *Here is the secret of inspiration. Tell yourself that thousands and tens of thousands of people, not very intelligent and certainly not more intelligent than the rest of us, have mastered problems as difficult as those that now baffle you.*
>
> —William Feather

If we were to assign various types of creativity to a hierarchy of values, puzzle-solving would not rank very high. Yet it is indisputably creative. We are provided with certain data and, through various well-thought-out or haphazard mental processes, we arrive at something that is new to us—a solution to the puzzle—or something that is very familiar, a wrong answer.

Arthur Whimbey in an article, "You Can Learn to Raise Your IQ Score" ° observes: "Many intelligent people score poorly in IQ and similar tests, not because they're stupid, but because they don't know how to use the intelligence they have. The evidence is mounting that scoring well on such tests is a skill that can be taught and learned." The five creative thinking skills can also be used to increase creativity in providing new and methodical approaches in solving problems and puzzles.

Whimbey offers this typical figural-reasoning problem from an IQ test: Instructions: The first four figures below change in a systematic manner according to some rule. Your

---

° Arthur Whimbey, "You Can Learn to Raise Your IQ Score," from *Psychology Today*, January, 1976.

task is to discover the rule and choose from among the alternatives the figure which should occur next in the series.

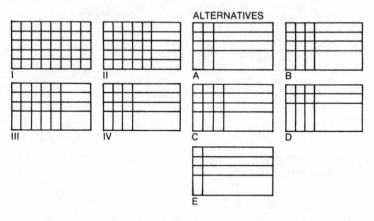

Figure 17

He explains that to solve the problem "one must compare the four figures. Each figure has fewer lines than the one preceding it, so counting the lines appears to be the next step. Alternative D is the correct answer according to the examiner." Obviously, he regards the problem as one of related structures or *order*. Yet a "college sophomore with an IQ of 95" could not solve this problem. She noticed that "lines were missing," yet when Whimbey asked her how many were deleted in the second figure, she said, "Three." "I asked her to count the lines again, and after what seemed like an inordinate delay, she said, 'Two.' Then I asked her how many lines were deleted in moving from the second figure to the third, and, again after much delay, she answered, 'Two.'" Wrong again. If one is viewing the problem from the standpoint of order, the girl's "errors" are incomprehensible. But, instead, when we look at them from a different, or *structured* point of view, there are three—not lines—but lines of squares removed in the third. Using the same "erroneous" reasoning, when two more lines of squares are eliminated in figure IV, one might—viewing the problem only from such a structural standpoint—find a shaky relationship of 3, 2, 2 and possibly 2 again. Therefore, Alternative B might be the "correct" answer.

Another student to whom Whimbey talked chose Alternative E, explaining "First there were some lines taken away. Then there were more lines taken away going the other way. Then there were more lines taken away going up and down. So I guess the answer should be take away more lines." From a simply relational point of view, Alternative E is a perfectly sensible answer. It is the same kind of answer you would get from a good cook who does not follow recipes: "Just the right amount," not so many vertical lines and so many horizontal lines but the one that "looks" right.

If we examined the problem from the structural viewpoint of squares, we would discover a mathematical relationship.

Differences in the number of squares within each figure:

Figure I   (40 squares) less figure II (25 squares) = 15 squares.

Figure II   (25 squares) less figure III (15 squares) = 10 squares;
              15 − 10 secondary difference (the difference between the difference) = 5.

Figure III   (15 squares) less figure IV (9 squares) = 6 squares; 10 − 6 secondary difference = 4.

Figure IV   (9 squares) less (unknown alternative) = 3 squares;
              6 − 3 secondary difference progression = 3.

This implies that V (the unknown alternative) must have 6 squares. The answer could then be either alternative A or D each with 6 squares, the progression of secondary differences 5, 4, 3 being the key to the answer. Are there then four "right" answers to this test question?

Certainly. And probably many other alternatives extending beyond the five choices. Are any or all of them right? Yes—with qualifications. The "correct" answer will depend on one's level and the point of view. Perhaps the greatest amount of intelligence required in an IQ test is used to determine the level and point of view of the person who devised the test. But it can only be assumed by the testmaker that if a problem is analyzed and equal weight is given to structure, order and relation, the "correct" answer will be discovered.

In this example, for instance, the person who made up the test viewed the problem from a two-dimensional standpoint: you are given a certain order (read "changes") and from that must discover a specific relation (read "similarities"). Also, you must ignore structure (read "differences") entirely, no matter how arbitrary that rule may seem. After all, the "solution" is, as Humpty Dumpty says in *Through the Looking Glass*, "just what I chose it to mean—neither more nor less."

Just how important a tester's hidden point of view may be is illustrated by the story that is told of the teacher who, in an examination, asked the question: How could you determine the height of the Empire State Building using only a barometer? That night as he graded the papers he found most of the students understood how the teacher wanted them to use a barometer as an altimeter: Measure the difference in the altitude on the ground floor and at the top floor. However, one boy said since he knew the height of the mercury in the glass tube was thirty inches, he would measure the shadow of the barometer and the shadow of the building and be able to find the height by triangulation.

The next day the teacher called the boy aside and said, "I would not feel right if I marked you wrong, but still you were not right. I was thinking of an aneroid barometer and you, of a mercurial barometer. Knowing that, how would you answer the question now?"

The boy immediately replied, "I would go to the top of the building and toss it off, timing how long it took to hit the ground. Then I would get the answer with the formula 32 ft./sec.^{2} and the number of seconds it took."

Teacher, "Again, you are not wrong, but still not right. Please try again, supposing you did not have a watch."

"Oh! Then I'd find the building superintendent and say, 'If you tell me the building's height, I will give you this barometer.' "

Puzzles and their solutions can be better understood by utilizing your creative skills in considering structure, order, relation, point of view and level—think of each one of these elements separately in attempting to discover the solution. Which one or group will provide a solution?

PUZZLES

1. Does the puzzle provide you with information about only the three skills and ask about the fourth and fifth? Gerald L. Kaufman in *The Book of Modern Puzzles* asks: "If you screw an electric bulb into the socket by turning the bulb toward the right with your right hand, which way would you turn the *socket* with your left hand to unscrew it while holding the bulb stationary?" Here you are given information about structures (the bulb and the socket) and order (turning) and asked to supply information about a new relation (similarity) between the bulb and the socket. You are also given irrelevant information about the old point of view, the right and left hand—irrelevant because it has nothing to do with the new sought-after change (order) and similarity (relation). The level in this puzzle remains the same. The answer is to the right. (The originator of the puzzle could have helped consider the reader's point of view if he had used "counterclockwise" instead of "right."

2. Are structure, order and relation changed in this puzzle? (Remember that when one is changed, all are changed.) Kaufman asks: "If you turn your right-hand glove inside out and put it on your left hand, will the palm of the glove be against the palm of your hand or the back of your hand?" Here structure, order and relation are *not* changed, only

viewpoint is. Therefore, the answer is, against the palm of your hand. (The original palm is inside out.)

3. Do the level and point of view you use allow you to see the structure, order and relation that are involved in the solution? If not, then *you* may be the problem and an approach is to change your point of view. This can be achieved by shifting to a different level where the structure, order and relation of the problem itself can be more clearly seen. New insights are then possible because you know what you have changed.

A) A monkey hangs on one end of a rope which passes through a pulley and is balanced by a weight attached to the other end. The monkey climbs the rope. What happens to the weight?

Solution: The weight rises like the monkey.

B) If you walked around the surface of the earth at the equator, how much farther will your head have traveled than your feet?

Solution: Your height times 2π. (6.2832)

C) If we had a string around the entire earth, which is 25,000 miles at the equator, and we added 36 inches to the length of the string, how much would this cause the entire string over the entire length to stand away from the earth?

Solution: Approximately six inches (using formula $2\pi r$).

Each of us facing life's puzzles may find the above puzzle-solving methods useful.

Here are a few world-famous riddles. See if one or more of the creative thinking skills would have assisted you in coming up with a solution.

1. Oedipus saved his life and prevented destruction of

Thebes by his ability to answer the Sphinx's riddle: "What walks on four legs in the morning, two legs in the afternoon, and three legs in the evening?"

Answer: Man: crawls as a child, walks upright in his prime and uses a cane in old age.

Riddles depend upon a creative approach for their solution, viewing a problem with a different concept of structure, order and/or relationship. The solution of the riddle of the Sphinx shows two skills viewed differently: order and structure. As to order, it viewed the time of the day as the same as the order of human life—the passing of time. If we look at time as an order of the day we could extend this concept by seeing the order of a person's life. Of course, the four, two and three refer to the person's walking ability. Structurally, we only viewed it one way, but when we looked at it as we might in another level, we saw that an infant crawled on all fours, in adulthood he walked on two and in old age, the evening, he walked with a cane. Using creative thinking skills in approaching these riddles is more rewarding than going around haphazardly trying to find a name like Rumpelstiltskin or the inspiration that might come to a few.

2. It is alleged that Homer was stumped by a riddle. It was presented to him by the fisherman of Los when they questioned Homer: "What we caught we threw away, what we did not catch, we kept."

   Answer: Fleas.

3. In *Alice in Wonderland,* at the mad tea party, the Mad Hatter's famous riddle went unanswered: "Why is a raven like a writing-desk?" Many inquiries were directed to Lewis Carroll to supply an answer. As an afterthought he wrote: "Because it can produce a few notes, though they are *very* flat; and it is never put with the wrong end in front!"

Since this was an afterthought, can you, using the creative thinking skills, supply some answers that would be appropriate to *Alice in Wonderland?*

I had recalled reading Carroll's after the thought answer. Rather than try to approach it on structure, order, relation, I decided to give it to the subconscious mechanism, and presented the problem to myself before I went to sleep. In the middle of the night I woke up and wrote down what had occurred to me, and read it in the morning. The following was the note that I made: "I don't know why a writing desk is like a raven and I'm sure the raven doesn't know either." The subconscious is famous for making humorous relations.

22

Inventions and Creative Thinking Skills

. . . well to beware that it be the reformation that draw-eth on the change, and not the desire of change that pretendeth the reformation.

        —*Of Innovations,* Francis Bacon

The man with a new idea is a crank until the idea succeeds.

        —Mark Twain

According to *The People's Almanac,* by David Wallechinsky and Irving Wallace, in 1912 Otto Titzlinger invented the brassiere. He was employed in a woman's undergarment factory and an opera singer complained about the discomfort of wearing a corset and the fact that the corset had no support for her huge bosom. This undoubtedly inspired him and he came up with a halter that provided support and added shapeliness to her chest.

The story unfortunately does not stop there: Titzlinger never received credit for the invention; he failed to patent it; many years later a Frenchman named Philip de Brassière took up the chest halter, added a little glamour to it and became immortalized as the inventor of the brassiere.

The story illustrates some valuable lessons for originators: protection and glory do not come automatically. The invention may not even bear their name.

But wait a minute. If you are a man, try a change in your point of view. You might see, as many women readers have already, that this story is too pat, too cut and dried, to be anything but a male-slanted story. Tested out, none of the encyclopedias seem to find "brassiere" worthy of mention. Webster's Collegiate, however, traces it back to an obsolete

French word for bodice. Larousse's French-English, English-French Dictionary disagrees. It says *brassière* in French means a child's bodice, and does not indicate that it is obsolete. It seems likely that Monsieur de Brassière is merely a euphemism—the substitution of an inoffensive word for an unpleasant one.

Then you might turn to the English-French section and find what the French call a brassiere. Well, the term in French is *soutien-gorge*. M. de Brassière is obviously not honored in his own country. Only English-speaking people use the term as we think of it.

Finally, you might consult Langenscheidt's German Dictionary. Certainly Germans, who are as chauvinistic as any, would not use a French name when a perfectly good Herr Titzlinger is standing in the wings. What do they call a bra? *Bustenhalter,* that's what.

After the fact, an invention is noted for its simplicity. Think of the carpet sweeper which combines a sweeper and a place to hold the dust, and takes the place of a broom and a dustpan. The safety razor permits us to use a razor at a standard distance and angle. The mimeograph applies ink to the paper directly as in block printing. Barbed wire uses wire in two ways: to separate an area with braided strands of wire and to deter animals from forcing their way through the fence with short, barbed strands of wire placed at intervals along the enclosing wire. The cotton gin was another simple invention: a comb to comb the cotton and a brush to brush the comb. Although Eli Whitney did patent this creation, that alone did not give him the protection he needed. Eli Whitney had to spend a good portion of his life in court fighting to protect his patent rights. The gin strengthened the South by making short-staple cotton profitable, and cotton became "King Cotton" in the South. Forced to accept very limited settlements for his patent right, Whitney then turned his attention to the manufacture of firearms. In his factory at present-day Hamden, Connecticut, he claimed to have originated the mass production line and the system of manufacturing interchangeable parts. (He stands alongside Colt.) For the initial protection of ideas we go back to the status of Monopolies of James I of England; enacted in 1624, it had a primary purpose of abolishing privileges and monopolies that had become a public scandal at the time. One of the exceptions made was of letters patented for the invention of new products. This was to become a part of legal inheritance of the United States and Great Britain. Today, inventions which are very special "good ideas" can be protected. They are the carrots of our culture, leading us to a new world: solving the problems of tomorrow with the methods of tomorrow. What young person has not dreamed of coming up with an original creation which will provide untold wealth?

Every ordinary product about us was once a new idea, an invention. When we take the time to examine these ordinary objects and consider them in reference to structure, order and relation skills, we can immediately see how the final idea (the point of view) was changing level and/or the combining or separating of structure, order and relation.

For simple relations, look at the paper clip. The fountain pen combines pen and inkwell. The pencil carries its own eraser. The safety pin carries its own clasp. Consider how certain discoveries were made when someone observed (order) change. For example, the fact that liquids expand when heated and contract when cooled led to the invention of the thermometer. The discovery of electromagnetic induction by Michael Faraday led to a change in levels and invention of the telephone, telegraph, and the generator and motor.

APPLICATION

Examine the above-mentioned inventions and classify their discoveries on the basis of how their inventor utilized the concepts of levels and structure, order and relation and ways they were combined and/or separated. For example, the carpet sweeper utilizes relation, combining broom and dustpan. Of course, order is also utilized in the action of moving the broom so that it can automatically collect the dust by a circular force of the broom (or brush) against the floor. Even a more creative solution has been discovered by the Japanese on a different level and point of view—don't dirty floors in the first place.

Continue in the same vein with each invention referred to in this chapter.

EXERCISE

Where Did You Fall Short?

Oscar Wilde: "I wish I'd said that."

James M. Whistler: "You will, Oscar, you will."

Most of us have at times tried to pass off clever remarks or jokes as our own. With certain inventions produced for the first time during our lifetime, we are reluctant to claim them as our own, but we may say, "Why, I thought of that years ago." Write down one or more of these "might have been" inventions.

Now analyze exactly what you "discovered." For example, take the electric toothbrush.

1. Was it structure? A toothbrush attached to an electric motor?

2. Was it order? A toothbrush that would change position, imitating a hand-operated brush?

3. Was it relation? Did you compare it with other electric cleaning devices that were more efficient than hand-operated ones?

4. Did you consider different points of view? Would some people consider it safer if it were battery-operated rather than plugged into an outlet?

5. Did you consider levels? Were you thinking of adults who are usually fairly careful about brushing their teeth or the children who aren't?

Choose one of your would-be inventions and analyze it according to what you did and did not do in considering it for the first time.

VII

Future Advances and Understanding

**The road built by one generation
is more willingly followed by the next
when shade trees and signs
are placed alongside.**

Gerard I. Nierenberg

23

Creative Thinking Skills—
Brain and Computer

John Von Neumann, one of the inventors of the games theory, once posed the question: Can you design a *system* (higher level) that will be reliable even if the components (structures) are not completely reliable? The answer, he decided, was yes—and the secret was redundancy. Herman Goldstine, author of *The Computer from Pascal to Von Neumann*, offers an example: Suppose you have three identical computers, each of which will make on the average one error in one hundred operations in the course of a long calculation. If you connect the three machines and require them to agree on each step before they go to the next, then if two machines agreed and the third disagreed, the two could reset the third at their agreed step and then proceed. Through redundancy (the higher level system), the chance of error would be reduced from one in one hundred to one in thirty three million.

I personally subscribe to the concept of the holistic brain, where experience is dispersed throughout. However, an interesting question is whether sections of our brain can act in a similar manner in checking against separate past experience. "The brain has the ability to relocalize functions after injury in the first two years of life, but not thereafter.

"The left hemisphere processes information sequentially

[*structure*]; the right hemisphere simultaneously, accessing several inputs at once [*relation*]. The left hemisphere works in series [*structure*]. The right in parallel [*relation*]."

"Our objective is to abstract patterns from Nature (right-hemisphere thinking) [*relation*] but many proposed patterns do not in fact correspond to the data. Thus all proposed patterns must be subject to the sieve of critical analysis (left-hemisphere thinking.)" °

Similarly, by comparing and changing our points of view while studying a problem, we can avoid serious errors and enhance our chances of finding creative solutions. Indeed, by changing point of view we change the structure, order and relation in our subjective world without being forced to also do so in the objective world.

As an aside, can computers be made more creative? Is it possible to improve the programming of computers and bring them closer to a "thinking" machine? Computers can very easily deal with a structure-difference and relation-similarity. However, order-change has been neglected. By integrating into the computer programming the order aspect of the creative thinking process, the "changing process" world will also be computerized. This would make such computers more "human." More simply stated: computers today are programmed with either/or alternatives which are frozen in for all uses. The world is constantly changing and so must the computer program to continually maintain invariance under transformation with the world.

° Carl Sagan, *The Dragons of Eden* (New York: Random House, 1977).

24

The Rewards of the Art of Creative Thinking

Capacities clamor to be used and cease their clamor only when they are well used.

—A. H. Maslow

The ever-changing world will continue to offer new opportunities to test and revitalize your creative thinking skills.

Do not allow the seeking of alternatives to be limited through premature judgment. Get your alternatives first, then apply your judgment.

When you have stimulated your thinking with these refound skills and generated large numbers of alternatives, be assured.

Although alternatives themselves will not give you a certainty of decision or confidence, they do permit you a wider exercise of your own judgment. In reflecting on many alternatives, you now have strengthened your own conclusions.

Continual practice will make you stronger and more competent. You will grow in interest, inspiration and talent. Your creativity will prove meaningful and successful.

CREATIVE THINKING SKILLS PROBLEM WORKSHOP—CONCLUSION

Now, after studying creative thinking skills.

Restate your original creativity problem (page 14 of the Introduction) in two lines, with attention given to the creative thinking skills of structure, order, relation, level and point of view.

Under the line you drew on page 14 of the Introduction, now add new solutions that occur to you after thinking specifically of solutions in terms of structures, orders, relations, and changing levels and points of view. Mark each new solution with "structure," "order," "relation," "level" and/or "point of view," where such skill was utilized.

Now compare these with the former thinking skills of structure, order, relation, level and point of view that were contained in your initial solutions in the Problem Workshop. This will permit you to discover any area that you were previously deficient in in your creative thinking problem-solving and indicate the areas for your creative growth potential.

Notes

Notes

Notes

Notes

Notes

Notes

Bibliography

Bruner, Jerome. *Beyond the Information Given,* ed. Jeremy M. Anglin. New York: W. W. Norton & Company, Inc, 1973.

Ferguson, Marilyn. *The Brain Revolution.* New York: Taplinger Publishing Co., Inc., 1973.

Gordon, William J.J.: *Synectics.* New York: Harper & Row, 1961.

Kagan, Jerome, ed. *Creativity and Learning.* Boston: Houghton Mifflin Co., 1967.

Koestler, Arthur. *The Act of Creation.* New York: Dell Publishing Co., Inc., 1964.

Korzybski, Alfred. *Science and Sanity.* Lakeville, Conn. International Non-Aristotelean Library Publishing Co., 1958.

Nierenberg, Gerard I. *Art of Negotiating.* New York: Hawthorn Books, Inc., 1968.

———. *Creative Business Negotiating.* New York: Hawthorn Books, Inc., 1971.

———. *Fundamentals of Negotiating.* New York: Hawthorn Books, Inc., 1973.

———. *How to Give and Receive Advice.* New York: Simon and Schuster, 1975.

Nierenberg, Gerard I. and Calero, Henry. *How to Read a Person Like a Book*. New York: Hawthorn Books, Inc., 1971.

———. *Meta-Talk*, New York: Simon and Schuster, 1973.

Osborn, Alex F. *Applied Imagination: The Principles and Procedures of Creative Problem-Solving*, 3rd Revised Edition. New York: Charles Scribner's Sons, 1963.

Parnes, S. and Harding, H., eds. *A Source for Creative Thinking*. New York: Charles Scribner's Sons, 1962.

Parnes, Sidney J., Noller, R.B., and Biondi, A.M. *Creative Action Book*. Charles Scribner's Sons, 1976.

———. *Guide to Creative Action*. New York: Charles Scribner's Sons, 1977.

Piaget, Jean. *The Construction of Reality in the Child*. New York: Ballantine Books, 1954.

Piaget, Jean. *The Moral Judgment of the Child*. New York: The Free Press, 1965.

Raudsepp, Eugene. *How to Present and Sell Your Ideas; How Creative Are You?; Characteristics of the Creative Individual; Motivating and Managing Creative Individuals; Conformity vs. Innovation; Why Be Creative?; Creative Growth Games;* Princeton: Princeton Creative Research, Inc. 1978.

Sagan, Carl. *The Dragons of Eden*. New York: Random House, 1977.

Tart, Charles T. *Altered States of Consciousness*. New York: Anchor Books, Doubleday & Co., 1972.

Torrance, E. Paul. *Creative Learning and Teaching*. New York: Dodd, Mead & Co., 1970.

Upton, Albert and Samson, Richard W. *Creative Analysis*. New York: E. P. Dutton & Co., Inc., 1978.

Upton, Albert. *Design for Thinking*. Stanford: Stanford University Press, 1961.

Weyl, Hermann. *Symmetry*. Princeton: Princeton University Press, 1952.

Index

riddle solving, 214-16
Rizzo, Frank, 182
Ross, John, 95

Sagan, Carl, 202, 226
salami strategy, 181-82
scientific method, creative thinking
    and, 112-16
Shakespeare, William, 21, 81, 117
Shaw, George Bernard, 77
Shulman, Burt, 158
similarities, relation and, 54-57, 62-
    63, 68-70, 71-72, 121-22
similes, 119
Sinnott, E. W., 19
Sophocles, 155
spontaneity, 21
Stakman, Elvin Charles, 181-82
Starr, Roger, 176
Stein, Gertrude, 36
Stewart, Kilton, 200-201
structure:
    applying skill of, 65-67, 78-80
    changing levels and, 53-54, 74,
        79-80
    creation of, 12, 22-26, 28-31, 39,
        40, 44, 45, 122
    general semantics and, 71, 72-74
    meaning of, 53-54

Sunderlin, William W., 56-57
surprise strategy, 175-76
synectics, 197-99

Taufaahau Topou IV, king of
    Tonga, 13
teleidoscopes, 44
Tennyson, Alfred, Lord, 85
Thomson, George Paget, 88
Thomson, Sir Joseph John, 88
Twain, Mark, 217

uniqueness, 71, 88-102

Von Neumann, John, 225

Wallace, Irving, 217
Welby, Viola, 118
Westinghouse, George, 172
Whimbey, Arthur, 209-11
Whistler, James M., 221
Whitehead, Alfred North, 112, 151
Whitney, Eli, 218-19
Wilde, Oscar, 221
Wittgenstein, Ludwig, 118
Wollman, Leo, 114
Wordsworth, William, 36

Yoshimura, Masatoshi, 17